How To Set Up
A Company
in the EC

How To Set Up
A Company
in the EC

Barry M. Sheppard

MERCURY

First published in 1990 by the Birmingham Publishing Company
New edition published in 1992
by Mercury Books
Gold Arrow Publications Ltd
862 Garratt Lane, London SW17 0NB

Set in Palatino by Phoenix Photosetting, Chatham, Kent

Printed and bound in Great Britain by
Mackays of Chatham PLC, Chatham, Kent

British Library Cataloguing in Publication Data is available

ISBN 1–85251–165–6

ACKNOWLEDGEMENTS

I would like to express my gratitude for information provided to:

- various offices of Price Waterhouse, especially Birgitte Tabbert (Denmark) Fernando Tanarro (Barcelona) and Sue Rees (Paris). The latter office can be contacted at 18 Place Henri Bergson, F-75008 Paris. Telephone (33-1) 42 94 45 45
- Sophie Elderenbosch at the Chamber of Commerce in the Netherlands
- the Department of Trade and Industry
- Companies Registration Office in Dublin
- Fionnuala Martin at the Irish Export Board
- Karl H. Horsburgh in the Luxembourg office of Deliotte Haskins and Sells
- Bente Smedegaard Neilsen at the Danish Commerce and Companies Agency
- Birmingham Chamber of Commerce
- Emmanuelle Eastley in the London office of Banque Nationale de Paris plc
- Mevr. M.B. Van Wijngaarden at the Royal Netherlands Embassy
- Svend Roed Nielsen of the Royal Danish Embassy in London

To Jackie, my secretary, who did a marvellous job with various drafts and understanding most of my handwritten notes, my special thanks.

To my mother – always there and always loved;
and to my son, Moysha, who has given me so much joy

CONTENTS

CONTENTS

INTRODUCTION

When I refer to a small business I do not mean it in any derogatory way. Basically, I regard it as a private limited company rather than a public company which offers its shares to the public.

Huge corporations can usually afford a multitude of advisers whereas you and I have to find methods of saving, thereby accumulating more money. It is for this reason that I have written this book: to help the smaller business save money and time in research. I feel sure that if you do not 'form' a business in one of the other member states of the European Community, you will at least be familiar with the type of business you are dealing with as we 'hurtle' along to 31 December 1992.

Make no mistake: 1992 is here and businesses throughout the EC are becoming more aware of the possibilities of openings for business in the other states. With so many different rules and regulations for the various countries my main purpose is to guide you in setting up a private limited liability company, or its equivalent, in any country of the European Community.

It's worthwhile here to start 'acclimatising' you to the different forms of public and private companies. The table will help you, at a glance, to see what type of 'company' you are dealing with:

	Public	Private
Germany	AG	GmbH
Italy	SpA	Srl
United Kingdom	PLC	Limited (Ltd)
France	SA	SARL
Spain	SA	SL

	Public	Private
The Netherlands	NV	BV
Belgium	SA/NV	SPRL/BVBA
Greece	AE	EPE
Portugal	SA	LDA
Denmark	AS	APS
Republic of Ireland	PLC	Limited
Luxembourg	SA	SARL

I have found that some countries' incorporation laws are very difficult. It is hard to find information, the address of the correct person to contact, etc. and then it is so spread and varied that you can only make certain assumptions.

My hope is that the less informative countries will look to their laurels: sort out their information and deal from one main office rather than leaving it to numerous officials. At the same time they should be looking at the prohibitive costs that can be incurred by someone seeking to invest time, energy and money in their country. They should be endeavouring to make it simpler and less expensive for a member state national to become involved in their economy.

I firmly believe that if the information costs are inexpensive, then it gives the entrepreneur more encouragement to open a business. He needs all his funds to build his company, not to form it.

In the UK it is not difficult to obtain a specimen memorandum and articles (in fact you could use the UK version in this book) as a basis for drawing up your own Articles of Association for the country concerned and either adding or subtracting items you may or may not need.

Whether you draw up your own articles or use a legal adviser, then I would strongly suggest that you always ensure that your area of activity (objects) is on as broad a base as possible and covers any eventuality that you think may arise. The reason for this is that if the objects need to be changed later, it is no easy matter to do so and it would also incur further costs.

Please do not think that I am biased; I have taken an overall view and found that the United Kingdom is by far the least expensive in which to form a company.

Harmonising Company Law

Company law is fundamental to the Single European Market and therefore it is an area where the Commission is very active. No less than twelve harmonising directives have been proposed; the UK has implemented five, and two more are covered in the Companies Bill.

Companies of Member States, like individuals, have been given the 'right of establishment' in another Member States by the EC Treaty. But giving effect to that right raises problems because the laws of Member States relating to companies differ, sometimes significantly. The UK and Ireland have particular problems because their laws are based on the common law system, whereas the rest of Europe follows the civil code system, with the result that the UK court's approach to interpreting laws is different from that of other European courts.

Originally, the Commission thought it was necessary to harmonise the laws to ensure that identical or similar safeguards exist for the protection of company members, creditors and other interested bodies. In the light of practical and political difficulty, the Commission's approach has changed over recent years with a move from harmonisation towards mutual recognition, i.e. what is good in one Member State is good in another! One practical result of this is that many simple business decisions concerning cross-frontier activities (even, perhaps, purchasing) may require a knowledge of more than one legal system.

It is useful to know how the decisions are made within the European Community.

The Decision Making Process

Briefly, the procedure is that the Commission may discuss a

[3]

proposal with officials from Member States and other interested parties before they adopt it as a formal proposal.

Once the Commission has adopted the proposal, it is submitted to the Council, the European Parliament and the Economic and Social Committee (ECOSCO).

A Council Working Group, made up of officials from Member States, then discusses the proposal in detail before referring it to the Committe of Permanent Representatives (COREPER) which in turn refers it to the Council.

Depending on the Article of the EC Treaty on which the proposal is based, Council can then either adopt the proposal, or agree a common position by qualified majority voting.

In the latter case, the European Parliament then has an opportunity to give a second opinion before the proposal returns to the Council to be finally adopted.

Once the measure is adopted and if it is a directive, as most company law measures are, Member States must implement it in national law.

If it is a regulation, it applies directly throughout the Community, though Member States may have to supplement it with national legislation.

The following are some of the proposals, etc. that are either being discussed, or in the process of becoming law within the Community.

The European Company

The Commission has proposed the creation of a new form of company based on European company law and expects it to be in existence by 1992. It is hoped that the European Company will encourage co-operation between companies within the Community, thereby allowing them to be more competitive and in a position to rival US and Japanese companies. Under the proposal, the European Company would be an optional form of company, limited by shares and governed by the European Company Statute. Such a company would be registered at the

European Court in Luxembourg and would be independent of national company law.

A European Company will be able to be formed only by a company which is incorporated under the law of a Member State. That company may be the ultimate holding company or a subsidiary of another company (including a non-EC parent company). For example, a European Company could be used to give effect to a merger between two companies based in Member States or, if they were forming a holding company, a subsidiary or a joint subsidiary.

The European Company would have:

- a two-tier management structure as proposed in the draft 5th directive.
- involvement of employees in the decision-making process, especially if such decisions concerned their jobs. The Commission in its proposal states that 'it is essential that the workers in the Community should be able to recognise the internal market as one they have helped to create and as one in which their interests have been appropriately safeguarded'.
- taxability of its profits only in the Member State where it is domiciled. The main tax benefits of such a company would be the ability to set losses incurred by subsidiaries in one country against profits made by a subsidiary in another country.

As it stands, the proposal for the European Company is bitterly opposed by the UK Government. The Department of Trade and Industry (DTI) doubts whether the considerable time and expense that will inevitably be required to adopt any new proposal are justified by the benefits that the European Company is designed to introduce. The DTI points out that many large-scale, cross-border mergers, associations and joint ventures take place already and ways have been found to get round the various legal and tax obstacles; so it questions whether the European Company will be used in practice for large-scale mergers, especially as it is optional, unless there are changes in the present tax régimes and takeover provisions.

The European Economic Interest Grouping (EEIG)

Since 1 July 1989 a new type of business entity has been available for cross-border trading co-operation, the European Economic Interest Grouping (EFIG). Based on the French Groupement d'Interet Economique, from the viewpoint of English law it is broadly a cross between a partnership and a company. The Commission's view is that as the EEIG is created under Community law and has effect in all Member States, it will encourage cross-border joint ventures: the parties will not be governed by the national law of one of them, thereby putting the other party at a psychological disadvantage.

An EEIG may be formed by natural persons, companies, firms or other legal bodies, provided that they are already engaged in economic activity within the EC. It enables two or more businesses to combine part of their economic activities, while preserving their legal and economic independence. An important feature of an EEIG is that members are jointly and severally liable for its debts. For tax purposes the profits of an EEIG will be deemed to be the profits of its members. An EEIG can be created with less formality than a company; all that is required is a written contract, but Community law prescribes certain details that must be included.

In August 1989 the first EEIG was formed by German, Netherlands and Belgian law firms. Its objectives include the support and development of the legal and economic activities of its members, and co-operation in the fields of law, science, trade and finance. (See also Appendix VI).

Abolition of Small Company Audit Requirement

The Commission proposes to do away with the requirement for small companies to be audited. This would affect nine out of ten UK companies.

Abolition could save small companies several hundred million pounds a year in audit fees; but the plan leaves little protection for those who trade with small companies. The DTI is concerned that other EC Member States will exempt closely held companies, namely small companies managed by their share-holders, from publishing accounts. This could cause problems for UK exporters and creditors who need such information to assess the financial viability of a company with whom they plan to trade. The DTI also says that the proposals will not reduce the burdens on small companies, because they will still have to produce much data for the tax authorities and possibly lending institutions.

Other proposals would exempt small companies from filing accounts with the Companies Registry. Accounts would be made available only to people who visit the company's premises. In a further Community proposal, companies of all sizes could be allowed to draw up accounts in ECUs rather than in their domestic currency.

The One Man Company

The draft 12th directive aims to create the concept of a single member company – something unknown in the UK, but already in existence in Belgium, Denmark, France, Germany and the Netherlands. The Community is committed to promoting the creation and development of small and medium-sized enterprises and this proposed directive is intended to encourage such enterprises. It will apply only to private companies limited by shares or by guarantee and the Commission expected the directive to be in force in all Member States by early 1990.

Disclosure of Branch Accounts

Disclosure requirements for branches of limited companies operating in one Member State but with headquarters in another country will be harmonised by the new 11th Company Law directive which came into effect on 1 January 1991.

Foreign branches of EC-based companies will now have to supply the accounts of their parent, prepared according to the rules of the 4th and 7th Directives. Branches of companies with their head office outside the EC will have to provide parent company accounts in equivalent form to those drawn up by EC companies. In cases where parent company accounts do not conform with EC rules, a branch will have to publish its own separate accounts.

Finally, where possible, I have included the formation articles. You will need to adapt these to suit your business requirements, but overall I think you will find enough information within the various chapters to write up your own articles of association, etc. for presentation to the appropriate authorities.

Unless you speak and understand the language of the country in which you wish to start a company, then I would certainly suggest that you use a formation agent – be it a notary, lawyer, formation agent or whatever.

I wish you luck.

Barry M. Sheppard

Note: The chapters that follow deal with each individual country: 12 chapters for the 12 states of the European Community. These chapters are not arranged alphabetically. I have put them in the order of their population figures.

1

GERMANY

Population	78 million
Capital city	Bonn
Largest cities (by population)	Berlin Hamburg Munich Cologne
Currency	Deutsche Mark – DM

Main holidays – 1992

New Year's Day	1 Jan
Epiphany	6 Jan
Good Friday	17 Apr
Easter Monday	20 Apr
Labour Day	1 May
Ascension Day	28 May
Whit Monday	8 June
Day of German Unity	17 June
Corpus Christi	18 June
Assumption	15 Aug
All Saints' Day	1 Nov
Repentance Day	18 Nov
Christmas	25 Dec 26 Dec

Business working days	Monday to Friday
Business hours	08.00 to 17.30
Bank hours	Various, generally 09.00 to 13.00 14.00 to 15.30
Vat rate	Low: 7% Standard: 14%

Types of Business Entity

Corporation – *Aktiengesellschatt (AG)*
The most advanced form of Germany company and the only one whose shares can be traded on the stock exchange. Foreign subsidiaries do not usually start with this legal form.

Private company – *Gesellschaft mit beschrankter Haftung (GmbH)*
The GmbH is the equivalent of a French SARL, the BV in the Netherlands and the Private Limited Company in the United Kingdom. The number of shareholders is not limited and share transfers can only be made with the consent of the other shareholders. Formation procedures are simple and documentation of shareholders' meetings and other internal matters is informal.

General partnership – *Offene Handelsgesellschaft (OHG)*
The OHG is a partnership formed on the basis of a partnership agreement as a self-accounting unit. Its members may be natural persons or legal entities but may not exclude themselves from the liabilities of the partnership. Net profits and losses are allocated among the members as agreed.

Limited partnership – *Kommanditgesellschaft (KG)*
Partners can limit their debts to the capital they introduce, but one partner must have unlimited liability; the latter is called the general partner. If the general partner is a GmbH, then the partnership is called a GmbH & Co KG. To obtain any benefits from a partnership, it is not uncommon for partners to form a GmbH to hold the general partner share. To this extent the unlimited liability can be worthless.

Civil law partnership – *Gesellschaft des burgerlichen Rechtes (GbR or BGB – Gesellschaft)*
This entity has neither a legal form, nor is it self-accounting. Its members agree to share in specific aspects of their own separate business pursuits. This construction is not normally suited to international operations.

Subsidiary of a corporation
A subsidiary of a corporation can be wholly owned and no investment or permits are required. There are no formation formalities and no restrictions on returning money (capital and earnings) back to parent company's domicile. A subsidiary cannot trade on its own behalf and must be in name of parent company.

Branch of foreign corporation – *Zweigniederlassung*
Can be either independent or dependent. If independent, must be registered at the Trade Registry and formally appoint a branch manager. If dependent, the foreign 'owner' is liable for the branch debts. This type of operation may have the advantages dependent on tax laws of the 'owner's' country.

Sole trader – *Einzelkaufmann*
Only natural persons acting on their own can be sole traders. This form has no relevance to the foreign investor.

Here we will be dealing with the GmbH where the owners are able to exercise personal control. Because of its structure and the ease with which it can be formed, the GmbH represents an ideal type of business format for foreign corporations wanting to limit the risk of their activities to the capital they invest in the Federal Republic and which do not anticipate raising capital on German money markets.

Rules and Regulations

Companies in GmbH form used to be governed by the GmbH Act of 20 May 1898. However, since no significant changes had been made since this law was introduced and the number of companies had grown considerably to over 350,000, 1980 finally saw a radical revision of the GmbH Act in the form of the Law to Amend the GmbH Act and other Commercial Legislation (4 July 1980 – BGBI 1 p. 838). The amendments came into force on 1 January 1981.

The GmbH is a capitalised company with a legal personality of its own. Its members participate by contributing individual shares to the original capital, but they are not personally liable for the company's debts.

Unless the GmbH Act contains stipulations to the contrary, the articles of association (hereinafter called the Statutes) may be liberally drafted so as to take into account the special needs and requirements of the company. In the past, at least two persons had to be involved in forming a GmbH; today only one person is required. The members of a GmbH may be natural persons, partnerships or other legal entities. The original capital investment must be at least DM 50,000. Each member has to contribute a minimum of DM 500, at least a quarter of which – not counting contributions in kind – must be paid in at the time of registration. Altogether, at least half of the proprietor's capital (DM 25,000), including contributions in kind, must be paid into the company.

In the case of a one-man company, the full contribution must be made immediately. However, a sole proprietor can make up the difference between his compulsory contribution and the minimum nominal capital by providing security (guarantee, etc.). If contributions are made in kind, a special report on the property must be presented so that its value can be checked by the registry court. If the stated value is found to be excessively high, the registry court is obliged to turn down the application for registration.

In order to form a GmbH, it is necessary to draw up the statutes in the proper judicial or notarial form. They must contain (in the German language):

- the name and head office of the company
- the commercial purpose of the company (objects)
- amount of initial capital (by each shareholder)
- date when articles are signed
- names of the Managing Directors/Directors, and indicate the appointment of a proxy

The company is formed only when the statutes have been entered in the commercial register at the local court.

The entry in the commercial register will be published in its entirety by the court in the Federal Journal (*Bundesanzeiger*). Everyone has the right to inspect the commercial register. It is not necessary to allege any special reason for doing so.

The entry itself:

- made at the local court (*Amsgericht*)
- in person or by mail
- in a publicly certified form
- can be registered by members of the board or by the business managers
- can also be registered by an agent.

Formation Procedures and Expenses

There are no special registration forms. The registration fees and the notary costs are based on the so-called goodwill (*Geschaftswert*) of the GmbH. To be included are the above-mentioned registration fees of the Commercial Register plus the costs for publishing the registration in the Federal Journal (*Bundesanzeiger*). Finally, there is a formation tax (*Gesellschaftsteuer, Kapitalverkehrsteuer*) of 1 per cent.

Summary of formation expenses (which are all approximations based on the share capital, e.g. share capital DM 50,000):

- attorney or notary public fees (DM 500)
- registration fees (DM 250)
- publishing the registration in the Federal Journal (*Bundesanzeiger*)
- formation tax (*Gesellschaftsteuer, Kapitalverkehrsteuer*) of 1% (DM 500).

Commercial Register

The basic facts about every business enterprise, and all changes thereto must be entered in the commercial register (item 8 et seq. of the German Commercial Code). Capitalised companies are subject to special rules in the corporation law and limited liability company law. Thus, for example, in making an entry for a GmbH, it is necessary to state the name and head office of the company, commercial purpose, amount of initial capital, date when the notarised statutes were signed, and the names of the business managers (item 10 of the GmbH Law). In addition, the entry must also indicate the appointment of a proxy, as well as the scope of the power of the representation possessed by the business managers of a GmbH or by the members of the board of directors in the case of a corporation.

The name of a GmbH must be derived either from the objects of the company or from the name of one of its members. It must always add the designation 'with limited liability' (mbH) to its company name. When choosing your business name (in your language) check to see if it would be offensive in German.

An agent may register the business if the terms of his agency expressly authorise him to do so. Such authorisation is inherent in a general power of attorney. An agency for commercial register entries must be publicly certified. The notary who has witnessed or certified the necessary declaration for an entry is himself authorised to apply for the registration.

What else do we need to know?

Shareholders

- Documentation of shareholders' meetings are informal, as are the other routine internal matters.
- GmbH are entitled to waive all formalities. Though resolutions must be in writing, it is sufficient to have them signed by the shareholders for validity. In fact, meetings do not even have to be held and also can take place anywhere in the world.
- The Director(s), sometimes called Registered Managers (*Geschafts Fuhrer*), can draft resolutions; shareholders sign them and return them to the company.
- Shareholders are only liable for their capital contribution.
- There is no limit on the total number of shareholders.

[15]

Shares
- Share transfers can only be made with the consent of other shareholders.
- Certain shares can be equipped with certain rights, for example, with a right of veto or with a right to appoint a Director.
- Share certificates (if issued) are registered. They are not freely transferable and are by notarised deed and they can also be subject to other conditions.
- Separate classes of share can be issued.

General – GmbH

- Membership of the local Chamber of Commerce is obligatory. The chambers will also help with any queries.
- Notice has to be given to the tax authorities after the GmbH is registered. The tax authorities will then allocate a tax number to the company.
- Ideal for foreign subsidiaries.
- Subject to corporation tax.
- Day to day management is entrusted to the Director(s).
- 100 per cent foreign ownership is allowed.
- The Director(s) must declare the GmbH bankrupt within 3 weeks if liabilities exceed its assets, or the company cannot pay its debts.

Management may consist of one or more persons whose appointment may be provided for either in the statutes or by agreement between the members. An appointment may be revoked at any time, without prejudice to any possible claims for compensation which the removed manager may have based on an existing employment contract.

The management is entitled to make day-to-day business decisions concerning the internal affairs of the company.

Meetings

The meeting of the members of the company is devoted to the

resolution of basic policy, presentation of the annual financial report, distribution of earnings, appointment and removal of management, amendments to the articles, etc. Decisions are made either at the company meeting itself or through the post. A member is entitled to one vote for every DM100 he had contributed.

To enable proprietors to monitor the management's actions, the GmbH Act gives each shareholder of the company an absolute right to demand information and examine the books. However, the right does not extend to information which would be used against the company's interests. A change in shareholding does not affect the continued existence of the company. A shareholder may be excluded for failure to pay his promised original contribution (the so-called forfeiture proceedings).

Since the reform of the GmbH Law in 1980, corporate bodies in GmbH form have been required by law to state their legal form, domicile, relevant commercial register and company registration number, as well as the names of their managers, directors and supervisory board chairmen, on company stationery and order forms.

Accounting Directives Law

On 1 January 1986 the Accounting Directives Law of 19 December 1985 (*Bilanzrichtliniengesetz – BIRIG*) came into force in which the 4th (1978), 7th (1983), and the 8th (1984) EEC directives where transformed into national Law. It involves to date the most significant harmonisation of company law in the European Common Market. The transformation of the above mentioned directives is to be found mainly in the Third book of the German Commercial Code; thus the first section contains such regulations (e.g. book keeping, etc.) concerning all classes of merchants (*Kaufleute*); the second section offers for the first time those essential regulations for corporations dealing especially with such matters as accounting (*Bilanzierung*), annual financial statement (*Jahresabschub*) and directors' report (*Lagebericht*). Also new is the classification of companies, in three sizes: large, medium-sized and small, which for obvious reasons allows the second and third categories to enjoy certain privileges, especially regarding the financial statements and reporting. (Small companies are, furthermore, exempt from the statutory audit.) Small companies are only considered in such cases when on two consecutive year-ends (*Bilanzstichtag*), not more than two of the following three requirements are exceeded:

- DM 3.9 million balance sheet total
- DM 8.0 million sales
- 50 employees (annual average)

Companies which are proved to be beyond the stipulated limits are defined as middle-sized. In order not to be classified as large-size companies, they are not allowed to extend beyond two of the following three requirements:

- DM 15.5 million balance sheet total
- DM 32 million sales
- 250 employees (annual average)

Large and middle-sized companies must produce their financial statements and their directors' reports within three months of the end of the business year. Small companies are allowed, on the other hand, six months.

In accordance with the *Bilanzrichtliniengesetz* (BIRIG) of 19 December 1985 (see Section 2a supra) the GmbHs are obligated since 1 January 1987 to publish their annual financial statement and directors' report as well as the shareholders' resolution for profit appropriation. For medium and large-sized classified GmbHs, the financial statement and directors' report are subject to statutory audit. GmbHs having control holdings of a certain size (*Konzern*) are not required to prepare and publish their group financial statements and directors' reports before 1 January 1990.

The audit is to be done by a qualified public accountant (*Wirtschaftsprufer*) except for medium-sized GmbHs which are permitted for the first time to refer to a certified bookkeeper (*vereidigter Buchprufer*). The shareholders must within the first eight months (by small GmbHs eleven months) adopt the financial statement and profit appropriations. As to the capital the *Bilanzrichtliniengesetz* differentiates between:

- issued share capital
- capital reserves (payments from shareholders)
- the revenue reserves

Also a further reserve must be formed for share surplus, unless the articles of association provide otherwise. Distribution of earnings takes place in proportion to the contributions of the members. Unlike the legal provisions relating to stock corporations, those governing GmbHs do not require that a reserve fund be maintained. Neither is it required that the annual financial statement be audited or published, except for those companies which resort to public financing and for this reason are obligated to disclose certain information to the public.

Company Searches

The Commercial Register (Handelsregister or HR) is designed to disclose all the important legal aspects of any business organisation domiciled in Germany. The HR is in two parts:

- HR 'A' includes Sole Proprietorship and General Partnership
- HR 'B' includes Stock Corporations – AG and Limited Liability Company – GmbH

Information that is available from the HR:
- business name
- the owner of a sole proprietorship
- the partners of a partnership
- mēmbers of the branch of an AG
- *geschaftsfuhrer* (M.Ds) of a GmbH
- incorporation
- capital increase
- liquidation and mergers
- special legal status of an employee (called *Prokura*).

Trade registrations in the HR are published in the Federal Gazette (*Bundesanzeiger*).

A GmbH can be brought off the shelf (*Vorratsgesellschaft*). The cost of this amounts to approximately DM 62,000, which includes the minimum capital of DM 50,000.

Useful Vocabulary

Acounting	Bilanzierung
Accounting Directives law 1985	Bilanzrichtliniengesetz (BIRIG)
Annual financial statement	Jahresabschub
Certified book keeper	Vereidigter Buchprufer
Chambers of Industry and Commerce	Industrie und Handelskammern
Corporations Act 1965	Aktiengesetz 1965
Commercial agent	Handelsvertreter
Commercial Code	Handelsegesetzbuch
Commercial register	Handelsregister or HR
Corporation profits tax	Korperschaftssteuer
Director	Geschafts Fuhrer
Employee	Arbeitnehmer
Federal Gazette	Bundesanzeiger
Federal States	Lander
Formation Tax	Gesellschaftsteur kapital-verkehrsteuer
German Federal Bank	Deutsche Bundesbank
German tax advisors	Steuerberator
Good will	Geschaftswert
Income tax law	Einkommensteuer-gesetz
Labour exchange	Arbeitsamt
Limited liabilities companies act 1892	GmbH – Gesetz 1892
Local authority	Ordnungsamt
Local county court	Amtsgericht
Management Board	Vorstand
Management Directors	Geschafts Fuhrer
Power of Attorney	Prokurist
Public Accountant	Wirtschaftsprufer
Regional Lower Courts	Amtsgerichte
Shareholders meeting	Hauptversammlung
State Central Banks	Landeszentralbanken
Supervisory Board	Aufsichtsrat
Testimonials	Zeugnisse
Value Added Tax	Mehrwertsteuer
Works council	Betriebsrat – BR
Year end	Bilanzstichtag

2

ITALY

Population	57 million
Capital city	Rome
Largest cities (by population)	Milan Turin Genoa
Currency	Lire

Main holidays – 1992

New Year's Day	1 Jan
Epiphany	6 Jan
Easter Day	17 Apr
Easter Monday	20 Apr
Liberation Day	25 Apr
Labour Day	1 May
Assumption	15 Aug
All Saints' Day	1 Nov
Immaculate Conception	8 Dec
Christmas Day	25 Dec
St. Stephen's Day	26 Dec

Business working days	Monday to Friday

Business hours

North	09.30 to 13.00 14.00 to 18.00
Central and South	08.30 to 12.45 16.30 to 20.00

Bank hours	08.30 to 13.30 14.45 to 15.45
Vat rate	Low: 2–9% Standard: 18% High: 38%

Types of Business Entity

Public corporation – *Societa per azioni (SPA)*
Is a company whose shareholders' liability is limited to the par value of their shares. It is similar to the US corporation and the UK limited liability public company. The minimum authorised capital stock (share capital) is 200 million lire which may be divided into shares of any denomination.

Private company – *Societa a responsibilitia (SRL)*
Is a company whose quotaholders' liability is limited to the par value of their quotas (shareholding). The minimum authorised share capital is 20 million lire.

Partnerships
- General – *Societa in nome collettivo (SNC)*
  Is a partnership where the liability of partners is not limited.
- Limited – *Societa in acconomdita semplice (SAS)*
  Is a partnership in which the liability of certain partners is limited, by agreement, to the amount of their capital contribution.
- Incorporated – *Societa in acconomdita per azioni (SAPA)*
  Is a partnership in which the liability of certain partners is without limit.

Joint venture
These are not specifically regulated, but Italian law provides for some kinds of contract that can be utilised for establishing joint ventures.

Branch of foreign corporation
A branch is established by registering with register of business enterprises in each place where located. There are no capital requirements and a branch may operate through its current account with its parent company.

Sole proprietorship – *Impresa individuale*
An individual can form a sole proprietorship as long as it is registered in the public register of companies.

Formation Expenses

The SRL is the type that most small businesses would be likely to
form. If you compare the costs of forming an SRL in Italy with a
similar type of company in the UK, you will find that there is a
huge difference. It appears that Italy is one of those countries
that encourage outside investors, but put huge costs in the way
of formation.

What do the formation expenses consist of?

- notarial fees
- registration with Chamber of Commerce
- registration charges
- Government licence
- authentication of company books (total)
- authentication of tax records

You will also have to consider the annual expenses as these also
are high. They consist of:

- Government licence
- Chamber of Commerce fee
- annual authentication (total)
- deposit of balance sheet and related procedures
- board of auditors (minimum)

To give you an example of the costs for formation and the annual
costs, I have referred to an article in *Il Mondo* dated June 1988.

Registration – SLR	Lire
Notarial fees	1,800,000
Chamber of Commerce subscription	24,000
Registration fees	200,000
Government licence	3,500,000
Authentication of company ledger	350,000

Authentication of tax books – each	25,000
Total	5,899,000
Annual Costs	
Government licence	3,500,000
Chamber of Commerce tax	306,000
Annual authentication charges (total)	150,000
Balance sheet filing/related formalities	96,000
Board of auditors (minimum)	
Total	4,520,000

With company capital up to 200 million lire.
If capital is over 100 million lire – payment to the board of auditors must be added.

Whatever your capital is, you have to pay nearly 30 per cent on top of that capital for the privilege of forming an SRL. Not only that, the annual costs are also very excessive – nearly 25 per cent, and even more if your capital is over 100 million lire. If after this you still decide to incorporate, then you must do so as laid down by the Civil Code and the company capital cannot be less than 20 million lire.

Formation Procedures

When choosing a name for your company in your own language, you should check to see if it would be offensive in Italian.

Two main documents are required for the formation of a SRL: the *Atto Costitutivo* (hereinafter referred to as the Articles of Incorporation) and the *Statuto* (Company bylaws) which contains rules concerning the inner workings of the company and forms an integral part of the Articles.

The articles of incorporation for a SRL must be in the form of a public deed and must contain the following information:

• name, date and place of birth, domicile, and nationality of each subscribing shareholder and the number of shares subscribed by him

[27]

- name of the corporation and the location of its registered office and branches, if any
- objects of the corporation
- amount of capital subscribed and of capital paid in
- number and par value of the shares
- value of contributions in kind, if any
- rules for distribution of profits
- number, names and powers of the directors, and an indication as to which ones have authority to act in the corporation's name
- number and names of members of the board of statutory auditors
- duration of the corporation

If there are any bylaws prepared by separate deed these are considered part of the Articles of Incorporation.

Procedure Before Incorporation

- Entire capital must be subscribed by at least two shareholders.
- Three tenths in cash must be deposited with a bank (returnable when the SRL has been included in the register of business enterprises).

The statutes must be deposited by a notary public (NP) within 30 days of being drawn up and then the Notary Public must deposit these at the Business Registry Office (BRO) at the district where the registered office is situated. BROs are found at the Legal Tribunal Court Clerk's Office.

But we have not finished yet; we need other documents besides the Statutes to go to the BRO:

- proof of deposit at bank (three tenths or more)
- appraiser's report – on the value of any contributors in kind
- any Government authority in accordance with any special laws – banking, insurance, shipping or air transport

Then what happens?

- The Court (BRO) then hears the opinion of the local district attorney.
- It makes sure the legal requirements have been met.
- It then orders the SRL's name to be entered on the business register.
- This last act gives the SRL its legal identity.

Once the SRL has its legal entity, it has to do a few other things:

- It must be registered at the local Chamber of Commerce/ Local Civil Court.
- It must publish the company deeds in the *Bollettiono Ufficiale Delle Societa per Azioni e a Responsabilita, and Limitata* (official bulletin for SPA and SRL companies).
- Must elect a Board of Directors and a Managing Director (if capital is more than 100 million lire, then a board of auditors must be appointed).
- Register for VAT (and have the records authenticated).
- If there are employees, register at the Tax Office.
- Register the names of directors with the Register of Commercial Companies and the Chamber of Commerce.
- Ensure that any director's name, address and nationality is placed in the register of Business Enterprises. The appointment must be published in official gazettes.

As you can see, the procedures before, during and after incorporation are very complicated.

What about shares and shareholders?

Shares, Shareholders and Meetings

- Shares may not be less than Lire 1,000.
- Each share carries the right to vote.
- The participants in an SRL are quotaholders. For ease of reference the participants have been referred to as shareholders, even though share certificates are not issued. These

quotas can be transferred either by contract or by testamentary (or intestate succession) provisions, unless otherwise provided in the articles.

- Shareholders' meetings must be at least once a year and the date must be within four months after the end of the financial year.
- Shareholder may appoint proxies.
- These proxies can represent at meetings, but such appointments must be in writing.
- Resolutions at shareholders' meetings must be entered in the minute book and signed by: the Chairman and the Secretary or a notary public.
- Extraordinary meeting must be drawn up by a notary public and entered into the minute book.
- Shareholders must be notified of procedures by registered letter.
- Amount of capital for majority:
  1st ordinary meeting   50% capital
  1st extraordinary   two-thirds capital

General – SRL

- It cannot issue debentures/bonds.
- Does not need a board of statutory auditors, if the capital is less than Lire 100 million.
- In companies without statutory auditors, every shareholder has the right to obtain information from the directors concerning the progress of the company's affairs and to inspect the company's books. Shareholders representing one-third or more of the capital have the right to have an audit of the operation performed yearly, at their own expense.
- It must have one or more directors (they need not be shareholders or Italians).
- The directors/employees cannot act as proxies.
- The directors' term of office is according to the statutes.

If you find that you need to form an SRL, then I would strongly advise you to go via a lawyer.

Useful Vocabulary

Annual registration tax	Tasse di concession governativa
Balance book	Libro inventari
Board of Directors	Amministratori
Co-operative banks	Banche popolari cooperative
Corporate income tax	Imposta sul reddito delle personne giuridiche
District Office of Direct Taxes	Ufficio Distrettuale delle Imposta Dirette
Foreign exchange control office	Ufficio Italiano dei Cambi
Inland Revenue Office	Intendenza di Finanza
Local income tax	Imposts locale sui redditi
Managers	Dirigenti
Manual workers	Operai
Middle managers	Guadri
Ministry of Finance	Ministero delle Finanze
Ministry of Foreign Trade	Mincomes
Ordinary credit banks	Banche di credito ordinario
Personal income tax	Imposta sul reddito delle personne fisiche
Police Authorities	Questure
Provincial VAT Office	Ufficio Provinciale IVA
Public charter banks	Instituti di creditor di diritto publico
Registration Tax Office	Ufficio del Registro
Residence visa	Permesso di Soggiorno
Savings banks	Casse di risparmio
Statutes	Statuto
Statutory auditors	Sindaci
Stock holders	Soci fondatori
Value Added Tax	Imposta sul valore aggiunto (IVA)

3

UNITED KINGDOM

Population	56 million
Capital city	London
Largest cities (by population)	Birmingham Manchester Liverpool
Currency	£ (pound sterling)

Main holidays – 1992

New Year's Day	1 Jan
New Year (Scotland)	2 Jan
St Patrick's (N. Ireland)	17 Mar
Good Friday	17 Apr
Easter Monday	20 Apr
May Day	4 May
Spring Bank Holiday	25 May
Orangeman's (N. Ireland)	13 July
Summer (Scotland)	3 Aug
Summer (not Scotland)	31 Aug
Christmas	25/26 Dec

Business working days	Monday to Friday
Business hours	09.00 to 17.00

Bank hours

England and Scotland	09.30 to 15.30
Northern Ireland	10.00 to 12.00 13.30 to 15.30

Vat rate	17½%

Types of Business Entity

Companies
All companies are regulated, governed and incorporated by the Companies Act 1985.

Under companies legislation, any two or more persons, associated for a lawful purpose, may form an incorporated company with or without limited liability. There are four types of company:

- private company limited by shares, where the liability is limited to the amount of share capital its members have agreed to pay.
- private company limited by guarantee, where the liability is limited to the amount its members have undertaken to contribute to the assets of the company, in the event of it being wound up.
- private unlimited company, where there is no limit to the liability of its members.
- public company, must be incorporated with a share capital of at least the authorised minimum, £50,000. Can raise capital by offering issues of shares or debentures to the public.

Partnership
Two or more people join forces. Like the sole proprietor, they are responsible for all debts. It is always best, if you decide the partnership route is for you, to have a formal deed that lays down all conditions of the partnership.

Co-operative
Individuals who have a similar purpose. They enjoy the benefits of bulk buying through the co-operative.

Branch of a foreign company
A foreign company may set up a branch in the United Kingdom and, once established, the branch may operate in the same way as a resident UK company.

The sole proprietor
This individual runs his business how it suits him, and takes all the profits or losses. He is liable for all debts incurred to the extent of his personal wealth, his business and any assets he may have.

The most common form of business entity used in the United Kingdom is the private company limited by shares (Ltd). It is similar to the French SARL and the German GmbH and the Netherlands BV. There are over one million in existence and in some years 100,000 or more are formed.

The Company Name

The formation of a company in the UK is quite straightforward and not expensive. There are a few formalities to adhere to before you start incorporating.

One of the most important is your choice of a company name. The registration of a name under company law does not provide protection against 'passing off' action under common law. Applicants are therefore advised, in their own interests, when applying for a company name, to check with names already on the register and, if necessary, seek legal advice.

When choosing a company name, it is particularly important that persons forming companies should satisfy themselves in advance on the acceptability of the proposed name, bearing in mind that an objection might be received to change its name. The Registrar does not give provisional name approval except in cases where the prior approval of the Secretary of State is specifically required.

Broadly a company name will not be registered if:

- it is the same as a name already appearing on the Index of Company names maintained by the Registrar of Companies.
- it contains the words 'Limited', 'Unlimited' or 'Public Limited Company', or their Welsh equivalents, or abbreviations of these words except at the end of the name.
- in the opinion of the Secretary of State it is offensive.

- in the opinion of the Secretary of State its use would constitute a criminal offence.

A company name will require the approval of the Secretary of
State if:

- The name would be likely to give the impression that the
company is in any way connected with HM Government or a
local authority.
- The name contains words which imply national or international pre-eminence, government patronage or sponsorship, pre-eminence of representative status.
- The name contains words which imply specific objects or
functions.

How to register a company name
Applicants are advised to check whether the name proposed is
the same as one already registered by reference to the Index
which can be inspected free of charge in the Public Search
Rooms of Companies House at Cardiff, Edinburgh and London.
In determining whether one name is 'the same as' another,
certain words and their abbreviations, together with accents and
punctuation marks, will be disregarded. These words include
the definite article and the words 'company', 'limited', public
limited company' etc and their Welsh equivalents, whilst 'and'
and '&' will be taken to be the same. Names which are phonetically identical, but not visually identical, will be allowed as not
being 'the same as'.

If the name is not the same as one already on the Index, and
does not require the prior approval of the Secretary of State, the
incorporation documents should be submitted to the appropriate Registrar of Companies. If the name is acceptable within
the provisions of the Act and the documents are correctly completed, the company name will then be registered and the certificate of incorporation issued.

For all names which require the approval of the Secretary of
State, applicants should seek the advice of Companies House,
either in Cardiff for companies intending to have their registered
office in England or Wales, or in Edinburgh for companies

intending to have their registered office in Scotland. Details about the requirements on the use of the name will then be sent to the applicant.

Capital

The minimum share capital is £100 and there is no upper limit. Subscribers need only take up one share each (minimum 2) of £1 each.

Formation Procedures

Once the name you have chosen has been checked, you can then proceed towards Incorporation. You have to submit certain documents and a fee to the Companies Registration Office.

Documents to submit

The following documents are required to be submitted before any company can be formed:

Memorandum of Association, which must show:

- name of company (name must end with Limited or Welsh equivalent)
- location of registered office
- objects of the company
- that the liability of members is limited
- share capital registered on incorporation
- number of shares taken up by subscribers
- witnessed signatures of the subscribers

Articles of Association

These cover the internal regulations of the company. The Articles can be registered with the memorandum in the case of a company limited by shares. If these are not registered, the company must adopt Table A as prescribed in legislation (Companies Act 1985).

Notification of First Directors and Secretary and the intended situation of the Registered Office (Form 10)

It should include the names and address of the first director(s), and the company secretary, together with particulars of other directorships held or previously held within the last five years. The address of the company's registered office should also be shown.

Declaration of Compliance (Form 12)

This is a statutory declaration made by a solicitor engaged in the formation of a company or by anyone named as director or secretary. It confirms that all the legal requirements for incorporation have been met. It should be signed in the presence of a person authorised to witness such a declaration and can be signed in front of a Commissioner for Oaths (a person in England who is authorised to witness such a declaration). The Commissioner for Oaths will only charge a few pounds to witness you signing the documents before you send them off to Companies House. It should not be dated any earlier than the other documents.

Specimens of these forms are in Appendix 1 of this book.

Fees

A standard registration fee is payable of £50.

Forms

The necessary forms for incorporation can be obtained from Stationery Section, PO Box 450, Companies House, Crown Way, Cardiff, CF4 3YA and The London Search Room, 55–71 City Road, London, ECY1 1BB (personal callers only). Specimen memoranda and articles can be obtained from law stationers, and this book.

Summary

As a summary, the following documents must be sent or delivered to Companies House:

- Memorandum of Association
- Articles of Association
- Form 10
- Form 12

These documents are then taken to the Commissioner for Oaths, who will witness your signature.

Enclose a £50 fee and send off all of the above to the Register of Companies.

Note Before you send these documents off to Companies House it is best to photocopy all of them for your records.

You now have to wait to receive your Certificate of Incorporation. When you receive this document, it will be accompanied amongst other leaflets by a booklet entitled *Notes for Guidance – The Companies Act, 1985.*

This booklet is a guide to the main requirements of the Companies Act 1985. It deals with the ongoing running of your company, including Directors' and Secretaries' responsibilities; Auditors; Company obligations; Accounts; exemption for small, medium and dormant companies; Company meetings; dealing in shares; printing requirements; and a list of 99 statutory forms that you may need for the running of your business. This list is very comprehensive.

I have not covered all of it in this book, because the aim of this book is to show you what you have to do to set up a Company in the UK. Whilst I deal with formalities on the arrival of your Certificate of Incorporation all the other requirements are dealt with quite comprehensively in the booklet above.

For your information, some of the main points are listed below.

Directors and Secretaries

- A private company must have at least one director.
- Every company must have a secretary. A sole director cannot act as the secretary.
- Any changes in the directors or secretaries or their particulars must be notified within 14 days to the appropriate Companies House on form 228.

Responsibility of directors/officers

The Companies Act provides for the imposition of penalties for failing to comply with the requirements of the Act. Directors and officers of a company are personally responsible if defaults occur, whether or not the preparation of returns, etc. has been delegated to accountants or other parties.

Section 730 and Schedule 24 of the Companies Act 1985 provide for a maximum fine of £2,000 for each offence of failing to file an annual return and for each offence of failing to file a set of accounts. On conviction after continued contravention, the maximum fine is £200 per day for each annual return and set of accounts. A director may also be disqualified from acting as a director or taking part in the formation or management of any company.

It is a criminal offence for an officer of the company to make false or misleading statements to an auditor.

Directors' report
The directors must make a report as part of the annual accounts.

Company secretaries' qualifications
The directors of a public company must take all reasonable steps to ensure that the secretary or each joint secretary of the company is a person who appears to have the knowledge and experience to fulfil all secretarial functions.

Section 286 of the Companies Act 1985 lists legal and other bodies whose members are suitable for appointment. However, the section allows directors flexibility to choose from other sources. This means that you (or your associates) can become the secretary but ensuring that the person elected as the secretary knows all the obligations of that position.

Obligation to show certain information

Every company, including all overseas companies establishing a place of business in Great Britain, must state the names of either all directors, or none (i.e. it cannot be selective) on all company business letters.

In addition, every company must show its full registered name legibly on all letterheadings, notices and official publications, bills of exchange, promissory notes, endorsements, cheques and orders for money, goods signed by or on behalf of the company, bills of parcels, invoices, receipts and letters of credit.

Companies are also required to show on business letters and order forms the place of registration as indicated by any one of the following: registered in England and Wales, London, Wales, Cardiff, Scotland or Edinburgh, together with the registration number of the company (shown on its certificate of incorporation) and, if the company is exempt from using the word 'Limited' as part of its name, the fact that it is a limited company. If a letterheading or order form shows more than one address, it is essential to indicate which is the registered office address.

A reference to capital is not obligatory, but if there is any reference to the amount of share capital on any company letterheading or order form, the reference must be to paid-up share capital.

Company name on business premises
Every company must paint or fix a sign (and maintain legibly), showing its name in a prominent position, on the outside of every office or place of business.

Registered office
Every company must have a registered office address. Details of any changes in the situation of a company's registered office must be sent to the Registrar on Form 287 within 14 days.

Company seal
Every company must have its name engraved in legible characters on its seal.

Disclosure exemptions
All companies must prepare full accounts for presentation to the members of the company. However, the following companies may deliver modified accounts to the Registrar.

Small companies
These may submit only a shortened balance sheet and abbre-

viated notes relating to it, if they satisfy two of the following criteria in any one financial year:

- turnover not exceeding £2,000,000
- balance sheet total not exceeding £975,000
- average number of employees not exceeding 50

However they must submit a directors' statement and a special auditors' report.

Medium-sized companies

These may submit a modified profit and loss account, which need not disclose turnover, a balance sheet and a directors' report, if they satisfy two of the following criteria in any one financial year:

- turnover not exceeding £8,000,000
- balance sheet total not exceeding £3,900,000
- average number of employees not exceeding 250

However, a directors' statement and special auditors' report must be submitted.

Annual General Meetings

Every company must hold a general meeting as its annual general meeting (AGM) each calendar year and there must not be more than 15 months betweem AGMs. Failure to hold an AGM is an offence.

Printing Requirements

It is important that documents concerning resolutions, memoranda and articles are of good quality. The following must therefore be printed:

- the original memorandum and articles of association
- any altered articles of association
- any altered memorandum of association

Most modern printing processes are acceptable. The print must be black on white paper of reasonable thickness (90 gsm).

Any plain typeface of medium or semibold appearance in either 10 point or elite (12 typewriter characters to the inch) can be used.

Only a top copy will be accepted, printed on plain paper and not on 'listing paper'.

Note

If you find that you would prefer someone else to incorporate your company for you in the UK, you will find there are formation specialists who will incorporate your company and check potential names, provide registered offices and so forth. The costs for these services are very reasonable when compared with other countries' formation costs.

Company Register

This can be purchased or, to keep expenses down, you could start with a combined loose-leaf binder to keep your records. It should contain:

- applications and allotments
- transfers
- mortgages
- debentures
- members names
- names of directors and secretaries
- directors' interests
- annual list of members, directors and secretaries
- minutes
- share certificate

Final Checklist

We now come to the final checklist. If you tick each item as you complete it, you will have an up-to-date record on the formation of your company.

1. Send off to Companies Registration Office for Forms 10 and 12.
2. Check availability of selected title.
3. Draft Memorandum and Articles of Association.
4. Fill in Forms 10 and 12.
5. Commissioner of Oaths to attest Form 12.
6. Send to Companies House:
   - completed Forms 10 and 12
   - registration fee £50
   - Memorandum and Articles of Association.
7. On arrival of Certificate of Incorporation:
   - order company seal and company sign
   - create or purchase the company register
   - order business stationery
   - make further sets of Memorandum and Articles
   - decide whether you need to be registered for VAT
   - hold first meeting of directors
   - issue shares
   - send off Form 88(2)
   - enter all relevant details in company register.
8. Commence business.
9. Within six months complete and return Form 224 (notice of accounts reference date) to the Companies Registration Office.

4

FRANCE

Population	54.3 million
Capital city	Paris
Largest cities (by population)	Lyon Marseille Nice Bordeaux
Currency	Franc (FF)

Main holidays – 1992

New Year's Day	1 Jan
Easter Monday	20 Apr
Labour Day	1 May
Victory Day	8 May
Ascension Day	28 May
Whit Monday	8 June
National Day	14 July
Assumption	15 Aug
All Saints' Day	1 Nov
Armistice Day	11 Nov
Christmas Day	25 Dec

Business working days	Monday to Friday
Business hours	09.00 to 12.00 14.00 to 18.00
Bank hours	09.00 to 16.00 Monday to Friday
Vat rate	Low: 5.5–7% Standard: 18.6% High: 33%

Types of Business Entity

Corporation – *Société anonyme (SA)*
The corporation or stock company must have a minimum capital of FF 250,000 if shares will not be offered to the public and FF 1.5 million if shares will be offered to the public. The minimum number of shareholders required is seven. Shareholders are liable to the extent of their capital subscription.

Limited liability company – *Société à résponsabilité limitée (SARL)*
A limited liability company has both partnership and corporation features. The minimum capital required is FF 50,000. There can be no public subscription of shares.

Single shareholder limited liability company – *Entreprise unipersonnelle à résponsabilité limitée (EURL)*
An EURL is a SARL with the sole exception that all the capital is held by a single individual or entity. The sole shareholder has all the powers normally exercised by the shareholders in the general meetings. Formation procedures and governing regulations are identical to those of a SARL.

Partnership
Silent – *Société en participation (SP)*
Silent partnerships do not have a legal personality and come in undisclosed or disclosed form. They may have either a civil or commercial purpose. Profits and losses are shared in accordance with the partnership agreement.
General – *Société en nom collectif (SNC)*
A general partnership is a legal person that has a commercial purpose. Each partner trades under the company name and the debts and obligations of the SNC are those of all the partners jointly and severally for an unlimited period.
Limited
There are two types of limited partnerships: those without shares, but limited by guarantee (*Société en commandite simple*) and those with shares (*Société en commandite par actions*). The managing partners have unlimited personal liability and the

[49]

limited partners are liable only to the extent of capital contributions. This type of partnership is not used very often.

Civil company – *Société civile*
Civil companies are partnerships that are subject to the civil law. They may not carry on commercial activities and are used notably for real property, agriculture, liberal professional, research and personal property management.

Joint venture
The traditional form of a joint venture in France is the silent partnership (see above).

Economic interest grouping – *Groupement d'intérêt économique (GIE)*
A second form of joint venture is the GIE, which is basically a joint venture with a legal personality and may be created without capital. In general, they are cost and not profit centres, and are normally used for exports, research and development pooling, joint sales, and purchasing or distribution agents for their members.

Branch of a foreign corporation – *Succursale*
For legal and tax purposes, a branch is not a separate legal entity from its foreign head office. There is no minimum legal capital requirement for branches of foreign companies.

Sole proprietorship – *Entreprise individuelle*
A sole proprietorship is managed under sole responsibility of an individual who is personally liable for business debts to the extent of all his business and personal assets.

Formation Procedures

In this chapter we will be dealing with the SARL, but before we do it is worth looking at a new company identity recently established in France and called the EURL, which enables only one individual or legal entity to form a company. All the regulations of incorporation, minimum capital required on incorporation, management, corporate purpose and cost of registration tax are the same as for the SARL. The main differences between the SARL and EURL are:

- Only one individual or legal entity is required for formation, but
  - an EURL cannot be sole shareholder of another EURL
  - a person may be the sole proprietor of only one EURL.
- A manager is classed as an employee.
- The sole proprietor, when acting as managing executive, is considered an independent professional.
- An EURL cannot be manager of another EURL.

A registration tax of 4.8% is payable if the EURL wishes to transfer into a SARL.

SARL

The law applicable to a SARL is the Law of 24 July 1966 and Decree of 23 March 1967. For incorporation the following are essential:

- articles of incorporation drawn up by legal advisors
- a bank deposit of legal capital under the company's name
- publication of incorporation in the legal gazette
- declaration of conformity – a deed detailing the proposed operation of the company and certifying that the shares have been subscribed and fully paid up. This document must be signed by all shareholders in triplicate.

The Articles of Incorporation and other documents must be filed with the Clerk of the Commercial Court and must be lodged at the Formalities Centre (*Centre Unique des Formalités*) located in the local Chamber of Commerce. The registration file must contain:

- two copies of the articles
- two copies of the deeds nominating the manager and the statutory auditor (if this has to be done)

- two copies of the declaration of conformity
- a report of the contribution auditor
- application for registration, indicating all the different elements of the identity of the company
- a copy of the request for notice to be published in the legal journal
- documents proving the identity and the commercial capacity of the managers and auditors
- documents verifying the type of contributions in kind, and the identity of the contributor

The SARL does not acquire a legal entity until the registration number is received from the Clerk of the Commercial Court at the department where it has its registered office (*Siège social*).
  Fees payable are:

- registration tax of FF 430 for cash contribution, 1% for contributions in kind
- publication in the legal gazette – approximately FF 4,000
- comercial registration expenses – approximately FF 2,000

The minimum legal capital is FF 50,000 which must be fully paid up on incorporation. All shares must be subscribed and issued and paid either in cash (*apport en espèces*) or in kind (*apport en nature*) at the time of incorporation.
  When choosing your business name (in your language) check to see if it would be offensive in French. The name should not create confusion with existing SARLs. Prior registration of names must be checked with the Patents and Trademarks Office (*Institut National de la Propriété Industrielle*).

Company Articles

The following information is required for registration of a SARL and constitutes the articles of the company:

- name, first name, residence of the prospective shareholders or their representatives acting by means of an exceptional power of attorney annexed to the articles of incorporation.

- purpose of the company (objects).
- company name.
- registered office: office address, amount of annual rental and address of landlord.
- term: maximum 99 years.
- share capital: minimum FF 50,000.
- share par value, number of shares. Allocation of the shares between shareholders.
- bank: name and address of bank where funds will be deposited. Date of deposit of funds.
- transfer and assignment of shares. The transfer of shares to third parties is restricted. It may also be restricted between shareholders.
- number of managers (*gérants*), no maximum.
- length of manager(s') mandate, no maximum; unlimited, if not provided for.
- first manager(s): name, first names, profession, residence, date and place of birth, nationality of the *gérant(s)* who must be physical person(s).
  the remuneration of the *gérant(s)* must be fixed by the shareholders.
  restriction of powers, if any: any restriction on the powers of the *gérant(s)* is not binding on third parties.
- fiscal year: dates of beginning and end of fiscal year.
- obligations undertaken by the founders on behalf of the company to be formed (if any)
- Acts which will become effective before the registration of the company (for example acquisition of commercial premises, signature of a lease, contracts etc).
- number of employees (distinguish between men and women, handicapped persons or apprentices under contract, if any).

Documents Required for Legal Formalities

For each manager
- birth certificate with mention of father's name and mother's

maiden name. Birth certificates must have been issued within the last three months when the application for registration is filed.
- residents' permit for EC nationals resident in France.
- if not an EC resident, a commercial card must be applied for (about one year to obtain).

For the company
- two receipts for the deposit of funds in the bank
- one original and one copy of the document giving the right to occupy the premises: title deeds, lease, rental agreement and proof of residence.

Shares

Because of the amount of detail regarding shares, shareholders, managers and general information, the main points are listed below.

- minimum par value of share = 100 francs.
- cannot be offered to the public
- *Parts Sociales* (shares as such) represent the ownership of SARLs (evidenced by deed) and are in the form of registered shares
- shares must be transferred by written deed (4.8% registration tax is levied on the market value)
- shares are freely transferable amongst the shareholders (unless restricted by the articles).
- shares cannot be transferred to outside parties, unless a 75% of the shareholders give their consent.

Shareholders

- A minute book (*registre des procès verbaux*) must be set up on special numbered paper, stamped by a judge of the

Commercial Court, for the minutes of the shareholders' meetings.

- There must be a minimum of 2 and a maximum of 50 share-holders, who can be individuals or legal entities.
- All shareholders' decisions must be taken at a shareholders' meeting.
- For approval of resolution at an ordinary shareholders' meeting, more than one half of shares is necessary on the first call, and a majority of votes cast on the second call. An extraordinary shareholders' meeting requires a majority of three quarters of shares to approve a resolution.
- Notice by registered letter is required to convene a meeting, a return receipt requested for a statutory auditor. Share-holders require a registered letter or notice in the legal gazette.
- Liability of shareholders is limited to contributions. Share-holders making an in-kind contribution are liable to the company for five years on the valuation, if the in-kind contribution was not evaluated by a statutory appraiser or if the valuation is different from the one given by the statutory appraiser.

Managers

- A manager can be appointed without holding shares in the SARL.
- A manager who is not a shareholder or who holds less than 50 per cent of shares is considered an employee. A manager who is a shareholder with more than 50 per cent of the shares is considered an independent professional.
- He or she is appointed by the shareholders for a fixed or renewable term.
- He or she can be removed by either a majority of share-holders or for legitimate causes by the French courts (at the request of a shareholder).
- Managers are empowered to distribute interim dividends

General (SARL)

Immediately after registration in the Register of Commerce and Companies (*Registre du Commerce et des Sociétés*), the SARL must set up accounting books according to the accountancy standard (*plan comptable*) laid down by the fiscal regulations of the Minister of Finance.

Apart from filing a declaration with various government departments (Finance, Social Security, etc), every commercial undertaking in France must be registered at the Register of Commerce and Corporations and notice of formation must be made known to the public.

The articles must be filed within one month from the date of the last signature at the office of the relevant tax authorities, i.e. either where the registered office is located or at the home address of one of the promotors.

- SARLs do not issue share certificates.
- SARLs must file copies of financial statements with the Clerk of the Commercial Court.
- Articles of Incorporation cannot be changed unless a 75 per cent approval of the shareholders is obtained.
- When the number of shareholders is reduced to one, a SARL can be transformed into an EURL.
- A SARL cannot be formed to act in banking, insurance, savings and loans or entertainment (except for movie entertainment).
- A statutory auditor is required when two of the following criteria are met:
  - total assets = FF 10,000,000
  - total sales for revenue before taxes = FF 20,000,000
  - number of employees = 50
- It is possible to transfer a SARL into an SA when accounts have been approved for at least two fiscal years.
- A SARL is liable to corporate tax.

Note:
Judging by information gleaned from conversations with business people who have formed a SARL (or are trying), it appears

that although in theory it seems easy to form a SARL, in practice it is very difficult. I know of a family concern which has been trying to form a SARL (they are English, but French residents) for over two months and they feel they are no further down the road than when they started. It is for this reason that I have included the French Articles of Incorporation etc.

Useful Vocabulary

Accountancy standard	Plan comptable
Board of directors	Conseil d'administration
Business tax	Taxe professionnelle
Clerk of the commercial court	Greffe du Tribunal de Commerce
Commercial registar	Registre du Commerce
Corporate income tax	Impot sue les sociétés
Creditors	Representant des créancies
Current assets	Valeurs mobilières de placement
Customs authorities	Direction Genérale des Douanes
General ledger	Grand livre
General Manager	Directeur genéral – DG
Independent appraiser	Commissaire aux apports
Legal and tax advisors	Conseils juridiques et fiscaux
Local tax inspector	Inspecteur des impots
Managers	Gérants
Minute book	Registre des proces verbaux
Patents	Brevets
Patents and Trademarks office	Institut National de la Propriété Industrielle
President of the board	President du conseil d'adminis-tration
Record of day-to-day operations	Livre journal
Registered office	Siège social
Registration taxes	Cour de Cassation
Residence permit (temporary)	Carte de séjour (temporaire)
Shares	Parts d'interet
Start-up expenses	Frais d'établissement
Statutory auditor	Commissaire aux comptes
Supervisory Council	Conseil de surveillance
Tax Authority	Direction Generale des Impots
Tax collector	Percepteur
Trademarks	Marques de fabrique
Work permit	Carte de travail
Value added tax (VAT)	Taxe sur la valeur ajoutée (TVA)

5
SPAIN

Population	39 million
Capital city	Madrid
Largest cities	Barcelona
(by population)	Valencia
	Seville
Currency	Pesetas (Ptas.)

Main holidays – 1992

New Year's Day	1 Jan
Epiphany	6 Jan
St Joseph	19 Mar
Holy Thursday	16 Apr
Good Friday	17 Apr
Easter Monday	20 Apr
Labour Day	1 May
Corpus Christi	18 June
St James	25 July
Assumption Day	15 Aug
Hispanidad Day	12 Oct
All Saints' Day	1 Nov
Constitution Day	6 Dec
Immaculate Conception	8 Dec
Christmas Day	25 Dec

Business working days	Monday to Friday
Business hours	08.30 or 09.00 to 17.30 or 18.00
June to September	08.00 to 15.00
Bank hours	
Monday to Friday	09.00 to 14.00
Saturday	08.00 to 13.30
Vat rate	Low: 6%
	Standard: 12%
	High: 33%

Types of Business Entity

Corporation – *Sociedad anonima (SA)*
A *sociedad anonima* (SA) is similar in all major respects to a U.S. corporation or a limited liability company in the United Kingdom; it can be either publicly or privately held. It is a legal entity whereby the responsibility of the shareholder is limited to the participation in the share capital of the entity.

Company – *Sociedad de responsabilidad limitada (SL)*
Very similar to the *sociedad anonima (SA)* and subject to the same general regulations but there are no shares, the capital being divided into participations. The maximum number of shareholders is 50 and the maximum capital is PTS 50,000,000.

General partnership – *Sociedad regular colectiva (SRC)*
General partners are individually and collectively responsible for their actions in the name of and on behalf of the partnership, their financial liability is unlimited.

Limited partnership – *Sociedad en comandita (SC)*
Limited partners have no power to act in the name of the partnership, their liability is limited to the amount of their capital contribution.

Joint Venture – *Union or agrupacion temporal*
The joint venture structure is available to foreigners doing business in Spain, but its use is generally restricted to specific types of business or to specific contracts to be formed in Spain. A joint venture can be with or without seperate legal entity.

Branch of foreign corporation – *Sucursal*
A branch or a foreign business entity operating in Spain is not a Spanish entity as in an SA or SL. A branch must nevertheless be inscribed in the Mercantile Registry. A branch may be used by the foreign investor when the activity contemplated is primarily commercial or as a prior step to establishing a more permanent operation.

Sole proprietorship – *Comerciante individual*

Joint accounts – *Curentas en participation*

Law
Commercial entities in Spain are primarily governed by the Commercial Code (*Codigo de Comercio*), which, although promulgated in 1885, still has general application. A series of laws, decrees and orders have modified but not changed the basic principles laid down in this code.

An SA and an SL are very similar in their legal formality and set up procedures. For this reason I shall explain the formation procedures for an SA and complete it by explaining the few differences between the SA and SL.

Formation Procedures – SA

An SA is formed under the Commercial Code and the corporation law (*Ley de Sociedades Anonimas, 1951*). The deed of incorporation (*escritura de constitucion*) must contain the statutes, which in turn must contain, among other information, the following:

- the name, objects, duration, and date of commencement of operations of the company
- the registered office
- the places where any branches or agencies are to be established
- the amount of the capital
- the number, par value, and class or series of the shares if more than one, and whether registered or bearer
- the unpaid portion of the capital and how the balance is to be paid up
- the structure of management and procedure for renewal
- the time limits and procedure by which shareholders' meetings are to be convened
- the procedure by which resolutions are to be taken.

Formation must be by public deed (*escritura publica*) before a notary. The public deed must be entered in the mercantile registry within one month of it being signed; thereupon, the corporation is a separate legal entity. It takes about two months to form a corporation.

Registration costs include a one per cent transfer tax on the registered capital, plus notary's and mercantile registry fees at scale rates. This amount does not include professional fees to submit applications to government ministries, draft statutes, and generally assist in preliminary negotiations and obtain tax advice, etc. There is no requirement for public disclosure of financial or other information.

There is no minimum capital requirement, but the total amount of the capital must be subscribed and at least 25 per cent paid up.

At least three shareholders are required to form a corporation, and there is no limit on the maximum number of shareholders.

The shares must have a par value. The subscription of capital can be by private or public issue. Shares may be issued for a consideration other than cash, in which case the amount and full details of the consideration must be stated in the deed of incorporation; or of the increase in capital, as the case may be.

Shares may be registered or bearer. Bearer shares are considered to be registered shares until they are fully paid up. A register of shareholders must be kept for all registered shares, and all transfers must be duly recorded therein.

There are two main classes of share, common and preferred; both must have equal voting rights. Shares may not be issued at a discount, but they may be issued at a premium. Share certificates must be kept in Spain, unless permission is obtained for them to be taken abroad.

Corporations may issue ordinary or convertible debentures, and long-term financing is available. Increasing capital by capitalisation of reserves is a common practice and for this purpose certain capital and revenue reserves may be used.

Shares are freely transferable, but all transfers, whether of registered or bearer shares, must be made through a stockbroker or notary public; the former is the more common and the less costly medium.

The liability of shareholders is limited to the amount of capital for which they have subscribed.

Formation Procedures – SL

An SL is formed under the Commercial Code and the company law (*Ley sobre Sociedades de Responsabilidad Limitada*) of 1953, as amended. An SL is limited to 50 shareholders.
Documents are called Certificate of Incorporation or Public Deed (*Escritua de Constitucion*). They can be obtained from a public service Registry agent (*notario*) and local lawyers. The public deed must contain:

- full name, civil status, nationality and address of the members
- company name
- objects of the company
- intended duration of the company
- registered office and location where the company will establish branches, agencies and other offices
- capital and participations into which it is divided
- goods, shares and cash that each member may contribute to the company
- appointment of directors of the company
- form of meetings and procedures for passing resolutions
- all other agreements and special conditions to which the members may agree

When completed they need to be sent to the Mercantile Registry (*Registro Mercantile*). All documents must be in Spanish (*español*).
Fees payable are:

- stamp duty or registration cost of 1% on the registered capital (*Impuesto sobre Transmisiones Patrimoniales y Actos Juridicos Documentados*).

- notary fees (*honorarios notario*) Ptas 42,000.
- mercantile registry fees.

An SL does not have shares; the capital is divided among the stockholders in accordance with their agreed participations, as set out in the public deed under which the company is formed. The maximum capital permitted is Ptas 50 million, which must be completely paid up at the date of issue. If a stockholder wishes to transfer his holding in a company, he must offer it to the existing stockholders. If they do not wish to buy, they cannot prevent the sale to an outsider. Changes in stockholders are laborious to bring about because a new deed must be drawn up. Stockholders may be corporations or other legal persons.

There are no restrictions on the use of names. Company name reservation is mandatory. Those already registered cannot be used. When choosing your business name (in your language), check to see if it would be offensive in Spanish.

You get a certificate to prove you have an SL from Mercantile Registry which must be displayed on the premises for trade and tax purposes.

Authorities who must be informed of the formation of an SL are:

- General Directorship of Foreign Investment (*Direccion General de Transacciones*).
- *Exteriores* (DGTE) – if capital contribution is made by a non-resident.
- Tax Administration (*Hacienda Publica*).

All legal entities must register with the Ministry of Finance immediately following their incorporation, and will be assigned a fiscal indentity number which is used for all tax purposes. Foreign entities which do not have a permanent establishment in Spain are subject to the normal corporation tax rate, currently 35% on income arising in Spain. This includes Capital Gains.

These formalities are usually completed by lawyers or legal representatives acting on behalf of shareholders.

The SL law was being changed in 1990/91 and standard documents are still under review. So we cannot give any specimen certificates, documents etc.

Directors and Other Officials

The Spanish company normally has the following officers:

- Chairman of the Board of Directors (*Presidente del Consejo de Administracion*)
- Directors (*Consejeros*)
- Managing Director (*Consejero Delegado*)
- Company Secretary (*Secretario*)

The powers of each are specified in the Bylaws or delegated in accordance with the Bylaws.

The shareholders appoint one or more directors as specified in the Bylaws to manage the company. Directors are not required to be Spanish citizens, residents or shareholders. Directors may elect a manager and delegate such power to the Manager as the bylaws permit.

Note: From my research I concluded that when setting up a business in Spain, it is very important that you use the services of a competent lawyer and accountant who have a good local knowledge, preferably have offices in your own country, have established offices in Spain and can correspond in your own language.

Useful Vocabulary

Balance sheet and statements	Inventarios y balances
Board of directors	Consejo de Administracion
Chairman of the Board of Directors	Presidente del Consejo de Adminis-tracion
Commercial code	Codigo de Commercio
Company Law 1953	Ley sobre sociedades de responsi-bilidad Limitada 1953
Company Secretary	Secretario
Corporation Law of 1951	Ley de sociedades anonimas
Corporate tax	Impuesto sobre sociedades
Deed of incorporation	Escritura de constitucion
Directors	Consejeros
Excise taxes	Impuestos especiales
Journal	Diario
Legal reserve	Reserva legal
Manager	Apoderado
Managing Director	Consejero Delegado
Mercantile registry	Registro mercantil
Minutes of meeting	Actas
Profit and loss account	Cuenta de Perdidas y Ganancias
Public deed	Excritura publica
Sales tax	Impuesto general sobre el trafico las empresas
Savings institutions	Cajas de ahorros
Shareholders	Accionistas censores de cuentas
Share premium reserve	Prima de emision de acciones
Sole administrator	Administrador union
Statute of the Workers	Estatuto de los Trabajadores
Transfer tax and stamp tax	Impuesto sobre transmisiones patrimoniales y actos juridicos documentados
Value Added Tax	Impuesto sobre el valor anadido
Venture capital companies	Sociedades de Capital-Riesgo
Voluntary reserve	Reserva voluntaria

6

THE NETHERLANDS

Population	14.7 million
Capital city	Amsterdam
Largest cities (by population)	Rotterdam The Hague
Currency	Guilder (Dfl or f)
Main holidays – 1992	
New Year's Day	1 Jan
Good Friday	17 Apr
Easter Monday	20 Apr
Ascension Day	28 May
Whit Monday	8 June
Christmas	25/26 Dec
Business working days	Monday to Friday
Business hours	08.30 to 17.30
Bank hours	09.00 to 17.00 Monday to Friday
Vat rate	Low: 5% Standard: 19%

Types of Business Entity

Private company – *Besloten Vennootschap met beperkte aan-sprakelijkheid (BV)*
This is the most common form of commercial enterprise in The Netherlands, and the one most frequently used by foreign investors. For practical purposes, it is the equivalent of a British Private Limited company, a West German GmbH or a French Sarl. The liability of shareholders (*aandeelhouders*) is limited to their capital subscriptions; the company is an independent legal entity that can enter into contracts and sue and be sued; and shares can be transferred (subject to certain restrictions) without affecting the continued existence of the company, although they may not be offered for public subscription or trading.

Public company – *Naamloze Vennootschap (NV)*
This is the form adopted by entities that wish to raise capital publicly, whether listed on the stock exchange or not. It corresponds closely to the public company or corporation form in most other countries. There is normally no restriction on the issue or transfer of an NV's shares or notes, although the NV's own constitution documents may introduce restrictions if so desired.

General partnerships – *Vennootschap onder firma (VOF)*
This is the usual form of commercial partnership, in which all partners are jointly and severally liable for all its debts and obligations. Partnerships are not legal entities separate from the individuals who compose them. The word '*maatschap*' literally meaning 'partnership', denotes a civil and not a commercial law entity, a form often adopted by professional firms.

Limited partnership – *Commanditaire Vennootschap (CV)*
In this form, the general partners are fully liable for the debts of the partnership, but there are also one or more limited partners liable only to the extent of the contributions they have made to the partnership's capital.

[71]

Branch of a foreign organisation – *Bijkantoor* or *Filiaal*
This is not a separate legal entity, but is an establishment of its
parent body, in whatever form that body carries on its business.

Joint Ventures – (same term used in Dutch)
Used not only for Dutch operations but to allow cooperation
between Dutch and foreign enterprises. The legal status can
vary from a partnership formed by two or more companies to
that of a separate company.

Co-operative societies – *Cooperatieve vereniging*
An association of persons that allows for the free entry and withdrawal of members. This type of business entity is frequently
found in such trades as agriculture and horticulture.

Sole proprietorship – *Eenmanszaak*
A sole trader does not have a legal entity and is therefore liable
for all obligations.

Formation Procedures

The BV is the one we will be following in this chapter. A BV must
be organised by one or more individuals or companies, who sign
the articles of incorporation (*akte van oprichting*, usually referred
to as *statuten*) before a public notary. (A notary in The Netherlands is a public official appointed by Royal Decree, whose
legally prescribed functions include drawing up articles of incorporation and deeds for the transfer of property and mortgages.)
A founder need not to be present at the signing meeting if he has
given a power of attorney to his representative or acts through a
nominee. A founder need not necessarily be a Dutch resident or
citizen. As a group, the founders must pay in a minimum capital
of Dfl. 40,000. Payment of capital may be made in cash or in
other assets. For each method of payment there are different
formal requirements.
    The public notary must submit a draft of the articles to the
Ministry of Justice to obtain a 'declaration of no objection' (*geen*

bezwaar). This declaration is given if the Ministry is satisfied that all legal requirements have been met. It may be refused only if:

- the background of the persons who will control the company indicates a risk of its being used for improper purposes or for activities that may harm its creditors
- the articles conflict with good morals, public order or the law
- the fee due to the Ministry of Justice for obtaining the declaration has not been paid

When the 'declaration of no objection' is obtained, the new BV comes into existence as a legal entity, with full rights. The founders then complete the incorporation process by registering the new company in the Commercial Register at the Chamber of Commerce for the district in which its legal domicile is to be situated; the total cost of incorporation must be disclosed at the same time.

The formalities required for incorporation usually take about two months. Consequently, a company is allowed to function on a provisional basis before the 'declaration of no objection' has been obtained, but must signify this by adding the initials 'i.o.' (for *in oprichting*, in formation) to the initials BV after its name.

A BV's managing directors are personally liable for its acts and obligations:

- while it operates on a provisional basis, and until registration with the Commercial Register at the Chamber of Commerce is complete
- until at least 25 per cent of the capital has been paid in (minimum to be paid in on formation Dfl. 40,000).

Registration in the Commercial Register is automatically reported in the Official Gazette (*Nederlandse Staatscourant*).

Unless the BV subsequently confirms the legal acts entered into on its behalf while it was still a BVi.o., tacitly or explicitly, its executives (in general the managing directors) will be personally liable for the fulfillment of its obligations.

Once you have incorporated your new company it must be registered with the local tax authorities, VAT office and the Social Security offices.

Articles of Incorporation

The articles, which must be in the Dutch language, set out not only the aims and objects of the company, but also its internal regulations; no separate document containing bylaws is required. The articles should contain at least the following items, of which some are prescribed by law and others represent general good practice:

- the company's official name
- the registered address, which must be in The Netherlands. The registered address need not necessarily be at the company's principal place of business
- the company's objectives
- if appropriate, the company's intended life. A company can be formed for a limited period, but more often is given an indefinite life
- the authorised, issued and paid-in capital, by number and nominal value of shares, expressed in guilders, including the amount of issued share capital of each type, if there are several types of shares and for each founder
- rules regarding the transfer of shares
- the powers of the managing director(s) and procedures to be followed if no managing directors are available, for any reason
- provision regarding supervisory boards (for enterprises that have such boards)
- the date of the financial year-end and rules as to the preparation of financial statements and audit
- rules for general meetings of shareholders
- shareholders' voting rights
- provisions for the appropriation of profits or treatment of losses
- dissolution procedures
- details of all pre-incorporation agreements that the new company will be required to assume; for example, those concerning the rights of the founders or contributions to capital other than in cash

Name

In the preliminary stages of forming a company, the founders must check that its proposed name is not identical with, or too closely resembling, the name of an existing company. This is normally done by the public notary through the Chamber of Commerce, which maintains a register of trade names.

The name must begin or end with the initials BV or the equivalent words spelled out, but otherwise it need not be in Dutch.

The company's name, registered address, registration number and location of the Commercial Register at the Chamber of Commerce in which information concerning it is recorded, must be stated on all its letters and order forms. Its name and registered address must also be stated on all other outgoing documents, except cables and the like and advertising material.

Costs of Incorporation

The chief expenses incurred in forming a company are:

- capital issue tax, which is charged at 1% on the amount of paid-in capital; where capital is contributed other than in cash, the tax payable on the value of the assets introduced
- the public notary's fee charged for drawing up and executing the articles of incorporation. For a company with an authorised capital of Dfl. 200,000, the fee would at present be about Dfl. 3,000. Additional fees are charged when difficult problems necessitate excessive correspondence, translation or discussion.
- Chamber of Commerce fee, charged for filing the company's documents in the Commercial Register. The initial fee payable at present by an enterprise with share and loan capital between one and two million guilders would be about Dfl. 1,300.
- Ministry of Justice fee, charged for issuing the declaration of no objection. This fee amounts to Dfl. 150.

Shares and Shareholders

The shareholders in a BV may be either corporate bodies or individuals, and in general any or all shares may be owned by foreigners.

Every share must have a par or nominal value. A BV may acquire its own shares, but not more than 50% of the subscribed capital; such shares have no voting or dividend rights.

All shareholdings must be in registered form and recorded in its share register. This register provides evidence of title, as share certificates are not issued by a BV. A shareholder may request an extract from the share register noting his own holding, but this does not constitute a document of title.

Types of shares issued are mostly similar to their counterparts in other countries. Ordinary shares (*gewone aandelen*) are the usual type, but preferred shares (*preferente aandelen*), which may or may not have cumulative rights, are also issued. Shares may be divided into fractional or subshares (*onderaandelen*).

Most importantly, the articles must include restrictions on the power of shareholders to transfer their shares, although such restrictions must not make transfer impossible or even extremely difficult.

Management

Except for the requirements concerning 'large enterprises', the law is quite flexible; it is possible for each company to adopt the form of management most suitable for its own operations.

Small companies often have only one managing director, who then functions as the company's internal operating manager and has complete authority to represent and bind it in dealing with third parties. A larger company may appoint two or more managing directors, and its articles of incorporation may stipulate whether one or more of them is authorised to represent it without restriction in dealing with third parties. In such a company, the managing directors may meet formally or informally

[76]

from time to time as a board of managing directors (*raad van bestuur*).

Managing directors need not normally be Dutch nationals or residents, nor need they be shareholders in their company. A corporate body can act as a managing director. Managing directors are appointed originally in the articles and, except in the case of 'large enterprises', subsequently by the shareholders' meeting, subject to rights granted in the articles.

Meetings and procedures

Management board meetings need not be held in The Netherlands, but when planning where executive control is to be exercised, thought should be given to tax questions related to residence. Briefly, if a company cannot establish that its management is actually exercised in The Netherlands, any tax benefits available (for instance, to holding companies) could be lost.

Normally, management board resolutions are passed by a simple majority of those voting; votes may be in writing or by proxy. Minutes should be kept to record such decisions. Loans to managing directors are not prohibited by law, but, if made, should, at least for fiscal purposes, be at arm's-length terms. Depending on the size of the company, information concerning such loans must be disclosed in the financial statements. The law does not require a director to disclose to the board any personal interest he may have in a contract to be entered into by the company, nor does it prohibit him from voting concerning such a contract. Provisions to this effect may, however, be contained in the articles or in a director's own employment contract.

Legal liabilities

Managing directors may be held personally liable for several reasons. Their liability may result from performance of their duties that is deemed unreasonable. They are then severally (each for the whole) liable to the company, unless any particular managing director can prove that he was not negligent.

Managing directors may also be held severally liable to third parties for their failure to comply with all the formalities for incorporation.

[77]

Shareholders' Meetings and Rights

In general, shareholders possess large, and to some extent, ultimate rights.

Shareholders' rights are normally exercised at the general meeting, which must be held annually within six months of the end of the proceeding financial year. Every general meeting (*algemene vergadering van aadeelhouders*) must be held in The Netherlands, although with the approval of all shareholders this can be changed. It is usually convened by the managing directors at the company's principal place of business or at a location designated in the articles. Shareholders are generally notified by means of registered or regular mail. Whatever means are used to call the meeting, 15 days' notice must be given and the business to be transacted must be described.

Shares of equal value must have equal voting rights and those of different value must have proportionate voting rights, so that the voting rights of shareholders are proportionate to the nominal value of the shares they own. It is possible, however, under the law for the articles, to restrict votes per shareholder under certain conditions. The articles cannot deprive a shareholder of the right to at least one vote.

Normally, a resolution is passed by a simple majority of votes cast. The articles may require a larger majority for special resolutions such as amendments to the articles, proposals to liquidate, or appointments or dismissals of managing directors when this is within the shareholders' legal competence. When the resolution concerns directors, the majority required cannot be more than two thirds of the votes cost at the meeting, representing more than half the subscribed shares. Other matters normally dealt with in the articles include quorum rules and adjournment procedures.

Shareholders may call special meetings, by obtaining the written agreement of owners of at least 10% of the subscribed capital (unless a lower percentage is stipulated in the articles of incorporation). Such a meeting must be called by the managing director within six weeks. If not, the petitioners may request that the president of the district court authorises a meeting called by themselves.

A shareholder who has a personal interest in a contract with the company may vote on any resolution concerning that contract, unless this is prohibited in the articles.

Proxy voting cannot be excluded by the articles, although it may be limited. Solicitors, notaries or accountants are often appointed as proxies. The articles may also allow votes in writing instead of in person; cable and telex votes qualify as well as those in written form. 'Out of meeting' resolutions must be approved unanimously.

Court Investigations

Shareholders representing one tenth or more of the subscribed capital, or of at least Dfl. 500,000 of the capital, may represent the court to institute an independent investigation into the management and general course of business of a company; for example, to protect minority shareholders. A trade union whose members are employed in the company, any other party granted such a right in the articles or in an agreement such as a trustee agreement on the issue of loan notes or bonds, or the Attorney-General of the Court of Appeal in Amsterdam can also request such an investigation.

If management is not cleared by such an investigation, it may face legal charges. In addition, the court may suspend or request the resignation of some or all of the managing or supervisory directors, or it may revoke a specific decision of the company. It is also within the court's authority to appoint temporary managing directors, to permit temporary departures from the articles of incorporation, or even to dissolve the company.

Petitioners must raise their objections beforehand with the company, or the court will not act. The company may defend itself against unfounded charges; unfounded complaints may result in substantial damages being charged against the complainants.

Share Capital

Dutch law recognises authorised, issued and paid-in share capital as three separate concepts. Shares must have a par to nominal value.

Because authorised share capital must be stated in the articles of incorporation, any increase requires an amendment to the articles; this can involve expense and delay. A company is usually formed, therefore, with an authorised capital of the amount likely to be required in the foreseeable future, but with a smaller amount issued initially. At least 20% of the authorised capital must be issued on formation, and of this issued capital, at least 25% must be paid in at that time. Partly paid in shares are not usual, however, and all issued shares are normally fully paid in without delay. Shareholders can always be held liable to pay in any unpaid proportion of their shares.

Payment may be in cash or in other assets; specific formalities apply to the different methods of payment. For payments in Dutch guilders before or on formation, a banker's declaration is required, stating that the money is available to the company. For payments in foreign currencies, the banker's declaration must also disclose the exchange rate at the date of the legal obligation to pay. Similar provisions apply to payments in foreign currencies after incorporation.

If the share capital, issued on formation, is paid in by means of other assets than cash, the founders must draw up a description of these assets, and an independent public accountant (a registered-accountant or in some cases an *accountant-administratieconsulent*) must declare that the value of the subscription in such assets at least equals the amount to be paid in on the shares. Under certain conditions, this requirement does not have to be complied with. If the share capital is increased after the foundation of the company, similar rules apply to payments in other assets than cash.

A company's capital must be expressed in guilders and the number of shares must be stated in the articles. Shares are not normally issued at a discount, but may be issued at a premium.

The legal minimum amount of paid-in capital is at present Dfl. 40,000; thus, this amount is also the minimum authorised and issued capital. Every two years the Government can change this minimum capital, in accordance with an official index number. If the amount of the share capital is less than the minimum requirement after a change, a balancing transfer from free reserves to a legal reserve must be made.

Losses
There is no requirement that liquidation is compulsory, if losses exceed any particular proportion of share capital. However, if a company continues to trade when insolvent, its creditors may be able to claim damages from the managing board if the company then goes into bankruptcy. Moreover, because of the rule that board members are liable to shareholders for the proper performance of their duties, the shareholders can also claim damages from the directors, if these damages are caused by negligence or by any impropriety by the directors.

Financial statements
The requirements for preparation, contents, audit and publication of a company's financial statements are complex and are described in detail in the booklet entitled *Taxation, Accounting and Auditing in The Netherlands*, available from The Netherlands Foreign Investment Agency.

Useful Vocabulary

Articles of association	De statuten
Bank reference	Bankverklaring
Board of directors	Raad van bestuur
Capital tax	Kapitaalsbelasting
Chamber of commerce	Kamer van Koophandel
Commercial register	Handelsregister
Corporate income tax	Vennootschapsbelasting
Declaration of no objection	Verklaring van geen bezwaar
Dividend tax	Dividendbelasting
Entrepreneur	Ondernemer
Inland revenue department	Rijksbelastingdienst
Managing directors	Direkteuren
Net wealth tax	Vermogensbelasting
Official Gazette	Nederlandse Staatscourant
Personal income tax	Inkomstenbelasting
Real estate transfer tax	Overdrachtsbelasting
Registered accountant	Registeraccountant
Share certificate	Aandeelbewijs
Supervisory board	Raad van Commissarissen
Supervisory directors	Commissarissen
Trade registration act	Handelsregisterwet
Trustee (administrator)	Administratiekantoor
Value Added Tax	Omzetbelasting – BTW
Works council	Ondernemingsraad

7

BELGIUM

Population	10 million
Capital city	Brussels
Largest cities (by population)	Antwerp Liège Ghent Charleroi
Currency	Belgian Franc (BF)

Main holidays – 1992

New Year's Day	1 Jan
Easter Monday	20 Apr
Labour Day	1 May
Ascension Day	28 May
Whit Monday	8 June
Independence Day	21 July
Assumption	15 Aug
All Saints' Day	1 Nov
Armistice Day	11 Nov
Christmas Day	25 Dec

Business working days	Monday to Friday
Business hours (can vary by half an hour)	08.30 to 12.00 14.00 to 17.30
Bank hours	09.00 to 15.30 Monday to Friday
Vat rate	Low: 6–17% Standard: 19% High: 25%

Types of Business Entity

Private companies – *Sociétés anonymes/naamloze vennootschappen (SA/NV)*
The capital of an SA/NV is represented by shares and, to the extent of their capital contribution, shareholders are responsible for the company's debts. Minimum paid-in capital is BF 1,250,000 in total and each issued share must be at least 25 percent paid in.

Private companies – *Sociétés privées à responsabilité limitée/besloten vennootschappen met beperkte aansprakelijkheid (SPRL/BVBA)*
Companies in which a corporate body is a member must have at least two shareholders, other such companies need only have one. The minimum subscribed capital is BF 750,000 and each share must be at least 20 percent paid in.

Partnerships
General – *Société en nom collectif (SNC)/Vennootschap onder firma (VOF)*
Partners are jointly and severally liable. General partnerships also frequently take the form of *association de fait/feitelijke vereniging*. These are de facto partnerships without the formalities of an SNC/VOF.
Limited – *Société en commandite simple/gewone commanditairevennootschap*
Limited partnerships are an association of at least one unlimited general partner and one or more partners whose liability is limited to their capital contribution and who cannot participate in management.
Limited by shares – *Société en commandite par actions/commanditaire vennootschap op aandelen*
These associations are similar to limited partnerships except that the partners' contributions are evidenced by shares.

Branches of a foreign company
A foreign company may freely set up a branch in Belgium. As

regards management and operations, these branches are subject to the same regulations governing Belgium companies.

Joint ventures
For joint ventures, no preliminary authorisation is required. For a public takeover or exchange offer, the person or company making the bid is required to file particulars with the Banking Commission before the bid is made.

Licensing and Registration

A wide variety of regulations covering business are imposed in Belgium.

Anyone who intends to set up a business in Belgium must prove that he meets all the requirements for engaging in that activity at the moment that the obligatory entry of the business is made in the Trade Register.

The requirements regulating the establishment of a business mainly emanate from professional bodies and are governed by nationwide laws. The national laws, in turn, are subordinated to the self-executory EEC Treaty provisions (Articles 52–66).

Besides registration in the Trade Register, the following may be mandatory:

- registration with the VAT authorities
- registration as an employer with the National Social Security Office; or
- registration as a building contractor when engaged in the construction sector of the economy
- opening of a bank account either with the Post Office or a bank represented in Belgium, in the name of the company in formation.

Prior to the formation of a company, an account in the name of the 'company in formation' must be opened with a Belgian bank. Each shareholder must transfer his cash contribution to this account, and the bank will deliver a certificate stating the amount of funds available to the notary who will sign the deed of incorporation.

Company name
The name of the company must be sufficiently different from any other corporate name in Belgium to avoid confusion, although no formalities are required to clear the name chosen.

Formation Procedures

The private limited liability company (SPRL/BVBA)
The SPRL/BVBA is a limited liability company, sometimes referred to as a close corporation, or a private personal company. This type of structure is commonly used by small companies whose shareholders are mainly individuals; companies are also permitted to be shareholders.

An SPRL/BVBA can be established by a sole individual, although in such cases special rules apply in certain situations (e.g. the death of the individual, where there is no partner to continue the business). A member generally is not responsible for company debts. There is restricted transferability of the members' shares, which are usually expressed in units, quotas, or fractions in the articles of association, or in riders to such articles, rather than as shares evidenced by issued stock certificates.

The procedure for setting up an SPRL/BVBA is quite simple. It can be summarised as follows:

- At least two founder-shareholders are required (if one member is a corporate body) but only one is needed if it is an individual.
- The founders must, prior to incorporation, submit to the notary responsible for the formation of the corporation a financial plan, justifying the amount of capital to be raised. The financial plan should include: a description of the company's activities; its estimated turnover and profitability; and estimated investments, loans, bank credits, etc.

[87]

- The articles of incorporation (*statutes/statuen*) and the bylaws must be signed by the founders in the presence of a notary. This must be done in Belgium. If the founders cannot be present at the incorporation meeting, they may be represented by authorised proxies.
- The articles of incorporation must be drafted, containing information as to:
  names and addresses of the shareholders
  name and address (which should be in Belgium) and legal form of the corporation
  amount of authorised capital
  capital subscribed and paid in
  number and type of shares (that is, whether bearer or registered)
- objects of the corporation
- duration of the corporation; (which may be unlimited or limited to a definite period)
- dates of the financial year-end and of the annual general meeting
- powers of the directors.

The company's articles must be filed with the Clerk of the Commercial Court and published in the Annexes to the Belgian Official Gazette. When the articles are signed, the corporation legally comes into existence.

Note: If bankruptcy is declared within three years after formation and if at the moment of incorporation the capital was obviously insufficient to cover the normal operations of a minimum two-year period, the founders personally may be held jointly liable.

Formation Costs

The cost of forming a company in Belgium can be estimated as follows:

The notary's fees are calculated as a percentage of capital according to the following table:

BF	750,000 to BF	1,500,000	0.8550%

BF	1,500,000	to BF	4,000,000	0.5700%
BF	4,000,000	to BF	9,000,000	0.3990%
BF	9,000,000	to BF	21,500,000	0.2280%
BF	21,000,000	to BF	71,500,000	0.1140%
BF	71,000,000	to BF	134,000,000	0.0456%
BF	134,000,000			0.0228%

There is a registration fee of 0.5% on the total amount of capital and property. In some cases, legal requirements connected with value added tax (VAT) are applicable. Cost of publication in the appendix to the *Moniteur Belge-Belgisch Staatsblad* is BF 2,400 + VAT per page.

For example, if the company is formed with a capital of BF 1,500,000, the cost can be estimated as BF 23,985. The breakdown is:

- BF 12,825 = notary's fees
- BF 7,500 = registration fee
- BF 3,570 = cost of publication of the articles in the appendix of the *Moniteur Belge-Belgisch Staatsblad* (three pages).

The formation process usually takes about one month. Any person or corporate body, Belgian or foreign, proposing to engage in any commercial activity of whatever kind, must first make application for enrolment in the commercial register. This is usually done when the notarised charter of formation is deposited with the clerk of the commercial court.

Shares

- Neither bearer shares nor bonds may be issued.
- The capital may only be represented by registered shares. A minimum capital of BF 750,000 must be subscribed, of which BF 250,000 must be fully paid in.
- Any transfer of shares must be agreed by at least one-half of the partners owning at least three quarters of the capital, except for the transfer of shares to other partners, spouses or close family members, or other persons specified in the Corporation Act.

Shareholders

- Shareholders' meeting must be held at least once a year.
- Majority vote is needed for resolutions, but can be by proxy.
- You can form your Articles of Association so that share-holders can vote by writing, facsimile, cable or telex.
- Meetings can be held outside Belgium.
- The company's powers are vested in the general meeting of shareholders, which delegates them to the board of direc-tors. The general meeting is also responsible for appointing one or more statutory auditors (*commissaries/commissarissen*) to report on the annual financial statements.
- An ordinary general meeting must be held at least once a year to approve the company's accounts, fix the allocation of profits, and relieve the directors and commissaire of their responsibility for the accounts submitted. The time and place of this meeting must be specified in the company's statutes. In practice, the meeting must take place within six months after the end of the financial year, as the accounts must be approved before the company's income tax return is filed; and this must be done within six months after the close of the financial year.
- Extraordinary general meetings may be called, and must be called if so requested, by the holders of 20 per cent or more of the capital.

General

- SPRL/BVBAs in which a corporate body is a member must have at least two shareholders, but otherwise it can only be one.
- A corporate body can service as a director.
- Small SPRL/BVBAs need only practise abbreviated forms of financial statements and is classed as such if the following apply:
  less than 50 employees
  turnover less than BF 154 million (excluding VAT)

balance sheet of less than BF 70 million
If, for instance, your company has a subsidiary then the parent company would be included in the above.

- Companies must be registered with the Register of Commerce.
- Directors/shareholders need not be Belgian citizens or residents, and foreigners can hold 100 per cent of a Belgian Company.

The consideration for shares issued must be in the form of cash or assets whose value can be appraised in cash terms. Any such assets must be described in detail in the act of formation and, in the case of noncash items, a company auditor (*reviseur d'enterprises/bedrijfsrevisor*) will be appointed to certify that the method of valuation is correct and in conformity with normal business practice.

Useful Vocabulary

Auditor	Reviseur d'enterprises/ bedrijfsrevisor
Belgian National Bank	Banque Nationale de Belgique (BNB)/Nationale Bank van Belgie (NBB)
Central registry office	Centrale des Bilans/Balanscentrale
Clerk of the Commercial court	Greffe du Tribunal de Commerce/ Griffe van de Handelsrechtbank
Corporation tax	Impot des Sociétés/ vennootschapsbelasting
Institute of Auditors	Institut des Reviseurs d'Enterprises/ Institute der Bedrijfsrevisoren
Local office of the commercial court	Greffe du Tribunal de Commerce/ Griffie van da Handelsrechtbank
Municipal authorities	Maison Communale
Non residents tax	Impot des non-residents/balasting der nietverblijfhouders
Personal income tax	Impot des personnes physiques/ personenbelasting
Statutory auditors	Commissaries/Commissarissen
Value Added Tax	Taxe sur la Valeur Ajoutee (TVA) Belasting over de Toegevoegede Waarde (BTW)

8

GREECE

Population	10 million
Capital city	Athens
Largest cities (by population)	Salonica Patras Heraklion Volos Larissa
Currency	Drachma (Dr.)

Main holidays – 1992

New Year's Day	1 Jan
Epiphany	6 Jan
Independence Day	25 Mar
Good Friday	17 Apr
Easter Monday	20 Apr
Labour Day	1 May
Whit Monday	8 June
Assumption	15 Aug
OXI (Rejection of Musso- lini's Ultimatum)	28 Oct
Christmas Day	25 Dec
Public Holiday	26 Dec

Business working days	Monday to Friday
Business hours	09.00 to 17.00

Bank hours

Monday to Thursday	07.30 to 15.30
Friday	08.00 to 15.00

Vat rate	Low: 6% Standard: 18% High: 36%

Types of Business Entity

Corporation or limited company – *Société Anonyme (SA)* sometimes referred to as *Anonymous Etairia (AE)*
The *Société Anonyme* was introduced to Greece by Law 2190/1920. Since then quite a few changes have been brought about by subsequent legislation, the major pieces of which are; the Legislative Decree 4237/1962, the Emergency Law 148/1967 'concerning measures to foster the capital market' and the Presidential Decree 409/1986, which harmonises Greek law concerning sociétés anonymes with that of the EC.

The concept of the société anonyme was introduced into Greece to facilitate the creation of self-supporting and viable businesses that would accumulate large sums for the development and modernisation of the country's commercial and industrial infrastructure.

The Greek SA is similar to the French SA, the British public limited company and the US Corporation.

Unlimited partnership – *Omorrythmos Etaria (OE)*
This type of company is defined as 'the union of two or more persons to carry out jointly commercial transactions'. All the partners are liable individually and jointly for the liabilities created in the name of the artificial person of the partnership.

Limited partnership – *Eterorrythmos Etairia (EE)*
What distinguishes this form of partnership is that in addition to the general partners who are fully liable for the partnership's debts, there are also limited partners who are liable only to the extent of their investment. On the basis of the contract of association there may be several limited partners but there must always be at least one general partner.

Shipping company
Law 959/1979 provides the legal framework for firms engaged in the shipping business, which plays such a major role in the Greek economy. The purpose of the shipping company is the

exclusive ownership, operation or management of Greek merchant vessels. To pursue this object, a shipping company may also participate in other shipping companies of the above law. The definition of merchant vessels does not include tourist, recreation vessels and vessels of maritime sports.

Branch of foreign corporation – *Ipokatastima Xenis Eterias*
Branches of foreign corporations and limited liability companies may be formed by a special decision of the Minister of Commerce. In general, there are no restrictions except that the share capital of the parent company should correspond to minimum capital requirements applicable to Greek companies and existence of reciprocity between Greece and the country of origin.

Limited liability company – *Etairia Periorismenis Efthynis (EPE)*
The EPE is similar to the private limited company in the United Kingdom and is the one to explore. It was introduced to cover the gap between sociétés anonymes and personal companies, and is governed by the provisions of the Civil Code, Law 3190/1955 as amended, Presidential Decree 419/1986 and articles 18–50 and 64 of the Merchant Law.

Law
Subject to the law, there is complete freedom to engage in business activities. This activity may be carried out by single individuals or by several persons acting jointly for the same purpose. The persons concerned may be either natural or artificial, and of any nationality.

In the case of a personal business, no particular legal form is required for its operation. Commercial companies are set up and operate according to the Merchant Law, the Civil Code or separate laws laying down particular forms for companies.

Formation Procedures

There are no standard forms for forming an EPE. It is done by notarised articles of association (sometimes called bylaws). The articles of association must include:

1. the given name, the surname and the profession of the members, their residence and nationality
2. the type and name of the company
3. the registered office of the company and its objects
4. confirmation of the capital of the company up to the required amount, the share of participation and the multiple corporate shares, if any, of each member. The capital must be fully subscribed with a minimum of Dr. 100,000 paid in
5. the contributions in kind, their valuation as well as the name of the member who makes such a contribution in kind
6. the duration of the company

The articles of association must be registered (within one month of formation) with the Court of First Instance by the Notary Public.

A summary of the documents of incorporation must be published in the Government Gazette and should include:

• members' names
• the Company's name
• its registered offices
• its capital
• the names of the managers
• the duration of the company
• the number of the contract
• the name of the notary public

Also every commercial and industrial entity must:

• register with its local chamber of commerce
• notify their local tax offices in order to obtain a tax registration number
• if staff are employed, register with the Ministry of Labour in Athens and with the local Social Insurance Authority

The articles of association must be signed by all the members before a notary public. The filing of the articles with the legal court and the publication in the government gazette brings the company legally into existence. Formation procedures are generally simpler and quicker than those for a corporation, although costs are broadly similar.

Minimum capital required is Dr. 200,000, half of which must be contributed in cash. The capital is not divided into shares, but into parts of at least Dr. 10,000 each. The part or parts allotted to each member are transferable, unless otherwise provided by the articles. Transfers are generally effected by notarial act and become effective when entered in the company's formal record of its members.

Two founders are required and these may be two or more natural or artificial persons, either Greeks or foreigners, whose liability extends to the amount of their corporate share.

Costs and Timing

Dependent on the size of the capital, costs of formation varies from 4 per cent to 6 per cent and consist of:

- registration tax of 1 per cent of the share capital
- notarial fees of approximately Dr. 15,000
- 1.3 per cent of the share capital for the Lawyer's fund
- Dr. 1,500 for copies
- Dr. 30,000 for publication in the Government Gazette

It usually takes 1 to 2 months to form a company.

Names

When chosing your business name (in your language) check to see if it would be offensive in Greek.

Shares

- No share certificates are issued, only quota certificates.
- Each share carries one vote and these shares are transferable unless Articles of Association (bylaws) forbid it.
- To increase/decrease the share capital needs a 75 per cent majority.

Shareholders

- Liability of shareholders cannot exceed the par value of their shares, unless those shares belong to one person or entity.
- The owners of the company are known as participation certificate holders and are responsible only to the extent of their invested capital. No stock is issued and participation in the capital may be represented by certificates, issued in the name of each investor, of not less than Dr. 10,000 each.
- The Articles of Association initially appoint the administrator(s). After this they are elected by the shareholders.
- Effective control of the EPE needs 75 per cent (of capital and number of shareholders).
- Routine decisions need a majority of both capital and number of shareholders.
- The following can only be initiated by a shareholder meeting:
  - any amendment to Articles of Association
  - annual financial statement approval
  - administrator – appointment or dismissal (and court action for removal).
  - profit distribution.

Required Business Records

The Tax Data Code requires all businesses and professional enterprises (both domestic and foreign) operating in Greece to keep business records and issue invoices and other documents. Failure to comply with this Code may result in fines, enforced termination of the enterprise, or criminal sanctions. Details of the shareholders are registered in a book which is kept by the Clerk of the Court of the First Instance.

Decision Taking

The members' meeting is the company's supreme body which

decides on every corporate matter and must meet at least once a year. The meeting nominates one or several managers, who may be members or third parties, to implement the decisions of the members' meeting and the smooth operations of the company.

The members alone can decide on matters of vital importance to the company, such as amendments to the articles, the appointment or removal of administrators, the approval of the financial statements, or the dissolution of the company. Resolutions may be passed by a majority of capital as well as of members. A meeting of members must be convened at least once every year within three months after the end of the company's accounting period. Members do not have to deposit evidence of their entitlement to attend as do shareholders of a corporation.

Reserves/profits
Every business year a sum equal to 5 per cent of the net profits of that year shall be deducted for the creation of an ordinary reserve. This obligation ceases when such reserve is equal to one third of the capital. The balance of remaining profits is distributed to the members in accordance with their percentages of participation in the company, unless specified otherwise in the articles of association.

Financial Statements

The administrators are responsible for preparing annual financial statements. Financial statements must be published in the government gazette and specified newspapers, but instead of being filed with the Companies Registrar they must be deposited in a separate EPE Registry at the Court of First Instance. Financial statements of small companies need not be audited.

Losses
The members of an EPE are debited with its losses, which they are expected to make good by paying in additional capital if the company's net worth becomes less than 50 percent of its paid-in capital.

Audit standards

There is no professional accountants' or auditors' body in Greece, and hence no requirement for Greek statutory auditors to follow the auditing guidelines published by the International Federation of Accountants. Independent professional firms with international connections, however, should observe their groups' international practices.

Other publication details

Any change in the articles of incorporation must be filed with the Companies Register at the Ministry of Commerce. The amount of detail required in the financial statements of small organisations is less than that for large corporations.

As a general rule, financial statements must be published within 6 months after the end of a corporation's financial year-end (normally 31 December, but sometimes 30 June or other permitted date). A corporation's first financial statements must be prepared not more than 24 months after incorporation.

The company's registered address and number must be disclosed on its business stationery. Additionally, the tax number allocated on formation must appear on all business documents.

Useful Vocabulary

Balance sheet analysis book	Vivlio apografon
General ledger	Geniko katholiko
General journal	Syngentrotiko imerologio
Income tax on corporations	Foros isodimatos anonymon eterion
Personal income tax	Foros isodimatos fisikon prosopon
Real estate tax	Foros akinitis periousias
Subsidiary ledgers	Analytika katholika
Value Added Tax	Foros prostithemenis axias

9

PORTUGAL

Population	10 million
Capital city	Lisbon
Largest cities (by population)	Oporto Coimbra
Currency	Escudo (Esc.)

Main holidays – 1992

New Year's Day	1 Jan
Good Friday	17 Apr
Freedom Day	25 Apr
Labour Day	1 May
National Day	10 June
Corpus Christi	18 June
Assumption Day	15 Aug
Republic Day	5 Oct
All Saints' Day	1 Nov
Restoration of Independence	1 Dec
Immaculate Conception	8 Dec
Christmas Day	25 Dec

Business working days	Monday to Friday Saturday morning

Business hours
  Monday to Friday
 	
  Saturday
	
	09.00 to 13.00
	15.00 to 19.00
	09.00 to 13.00

Bank hours	08.30 to 11.45 13.00 to 14.45
Vat rate	Low: 0–8% Standard: 17% High: 30%

Types of Business Entity

Corporation – *Sociedade Anonima (SA)*
- A corporation is formed when its statutes are signed by the founders at a Portuguese notary and after its commercial registration.
- The statutes must be published in Diario de Republica.
- A Certificate issued by *Registo Nacional das Passoas Colectivas* is necessary proving the non-existence of any partnership with the same or a similar name to the one intended to be used.
- The minimum equity capital is Esc. 5,000,000.
- Shares must have a minimum of Esc. 1,000. This is no upper limit to the number of shareholders, the minimum allowed is 5.
- Each shareholder's liability is limited to the value of shares subscribed.

Company – *Sociedade por quotas (LDA)*
- Similar to a corporation except that companies cannot be formed by public subscription.
- The minimum equity capital is Esc. 400,000.
- Shares must have a minimum of Esc. 20,000.
- Must have at least two shareholders.
- Shareholders are jointly liable for all financing stipulated in the articles of association. Only the company's assets can meet the company's debts with creditors.

Limited liability single-shareholder company – *Estabelecimento Individual de Responsabilidade Limitada (EIRL)*
- The allocation of a portion of a trader's, industrialist's or farmer's assets for the purposes of setting up a company where the investor's liability is restricted to the allocation portion.
- The company is formed by act of notary public and must subsequently be recorded with the Registrar of Commercial Companies. The notary is responsible for publishing the company's statutes in the official government gazette.

- Capital is always shown in Escudos and not less than Esc. 400,000.
- Only the establishment's assets will meet, in principle, the debts incurred in the course of business.

Branches – *Sucursals*
- Branches are set up by registering with the Registrar of Companies (*Conservatoria do Registo Comercial*) in the area where the branch is to be situated. The Registrar takes note of the essential elements of the articles of association, including the capital invested, and the powers of the directors/managers. By establishing a branch, a company is able to conduct normal business affairs through the branch which, however, does not have its own separate legal standing.
- There are no limits on the amount of capital needed for setting up branches and the company is free to decide on what the capital needs of its branches are.
- The branch may not assume any legal responsibility for its activities which are instead the responsibility of the company's head office.

Formation Procedures

The LDA is the most convenient form for small and medium-sized enterprises, but firstly let me say this is extremely complicated, time-consuming and costly. The necessary steps to be taken in order to set up and legalise a company in Portugal are basically as follows.

There is a minimum requirement of two founder members who need to contact The Portuguese Foreign Trade Institute (IECP), for the 'Previous Declaration' (Form A) of foreign investment in Portugal. This allows the importation of the capital with which the foreigner(s) will invest in their company.

You now need to create the Companies Articles which should contain:

- names or company names of all founding parties together with their addresses and nationality

- the company name and head office address
- objects of the company
- duration of the company
- capital shares and nature of each party's share
- description of shares other than cash.

You then choose a name for the company. You have to obtain authorisation of the company name from the *Registo Nacional de Pessoas Colectivas* (Form 31). All parts of the company name have to be in Portuguese with the exception of those foreign words or parts of words or fashion which are authorised by law.

You will need to deposit the minimum legal capital stock (at least half) in a bank account in the name of the yet to be subscribed company. Then obtain identity cards for the shareholders.

The company's deed (Memorandum and Articles) when approved is published in the Official Gazette (*Diario da Republic*) and the local newspaper. Before you can do this you must present to a notary:

- certificate of admission of company name
- bank statement proving the deposit of cash
- company articles
- identity cards for the shareholders

After this you register the company with the local Commercial Registration Office (*Conservatoria do Registo Commercial*). You also have to obtain a Certificate of Registration and Commencement of Commercial Activity from the revenue office in the district where the company is located.

You then deposit, again with the RNPC:

- a legal copy of the deed
- a copy of the Government Bulletin in which the deed was published

It is then necessary to register with the local trade offices the above documents and also:

- a copy of the newspaper in which the deed was published
- a copy of admission of company name

[107]

- the provisional identification card
- a copy of certificate of commencement of activity

Then apply for the company's definite identity card, which works as its fiscal number. To get this you show your certificate proving registration with the trade office (as above).

It is then necessary to register:

- with the local Fiscal Office; this procedure is called *Declaracao de Inicio de Actividade*
- all labour contracts with foreign employees with the *Minieterio de Emprego e da Seguranca Social*
- the company and employees with the Social Security department
- the official books with the tax authorities, civil court and bankruptcy office and obtain legal certification of the company's accounting books.

You must also obtain authorisation for office hours and file a declaration of start of activities with the local tax authorities.

Formation Expenses

Each time you deal with one of the various offices, there is a fee payable for each transaction. These costs can vary, but basically they are:

- stamp tax – 1% of subscribed capital
- notarial fee – Esc. 1,000 for the Company Deed, plus an additional Esc. 100 per page.
  A sliding scale of supplementary fees based on each Esc. 1,000 of capital, or a fraction thereof, must be paid as follows:

up to Esc. 200,000	10 Esc.
Esc. 200,000 to 1,000,000	5 Esc.
Esc. 1,000,000 to 10,000,000	4 Esc.
over Esc. 10,000,000	3 Esc.

  An additional 30 per cent surcharge is added where the company is being newly formed.

- Registration fees with the Commercial Registry of Esc. 1,000. A further fee of 1,500 is payable on registering the Company Deed, plus variable charges depending on the capitalisation in accordance with the above scale of notarial fees.
- Esc. 1,000 for requesting certification of approval for the company name with the National Registry of Collective Persons plus Esc. 3,000 when approval certificate is issued.

Registration procedure usually takes eight to ten weeks.

Guarantees Given to Foreign Investors

When establishing a business in Portugal, foreign investors will benefit from a range of guarantees and, as a general principle, are not objects of discrimination vis-à-vis the Portuguese entrepreneurs. The Portguese state guarantees the safety and protection of goods and rights resulting from foreign investment.

Under the terms of foreign exchange legislation, foreign investors have the right to transfer abroad:

- dividends or distributed profits, after legal deductions and taxes due and taking into account their participation in the company's equity
- the proceeds of settlement of their investments, including capital gains, after payment of taxes due
- any amounts due after deduction of relevant taxes foreseen in deeds or contracts regarded as foreign investment.

I would strongly advice that in Portugal you use a Public Notary for the formation of your LDA. As you can see from the above it is a very involved process.

Useful Vocabulary

Articles of association	Estatutos
Balance sheet	Balanço, balancete
Current account	Conta corrente
(with interest)	(com juros)
Foreign investment	Instituto de Investimento
Institute	Estrangeior
Government Gazette	Diario da Republica
Income tax	Imposto sôbre a renda
Information Bulletin	Boletim de Informacão
Managers	Gerentes
Ministry of Labour, Industry and	Ministério de Traballo, Indústria e
Commerce	Comércio
Official Gazette	Memorial
Register of Companies	Conservatoria do Registo
	Comercial
State savings bank	Caix a econômica
Statutes	Estatutos
Statutory auditor	Legal ouvinte
Stock	Capital comercial

10

DENMARK

Population	5.1 million
Capital city	Copenhagen
Largest cities (by population)	Arhus Odense Aalborg
Currency	Krone (Kr)

Main holidays – 1992

New Year's Day	1 Jan
Maundy Thursday	16 Apr
Good Friday	17 Apr
Easter Monday	20 Apr
General Prayer Day	15 May
Ascension Day	28 May
Constitution Day	5 June
Whit Monday	8 June
Christmas Day	25 Dec
Boxing Day	26 Dec

Business working days	Monday to Friday
Business hours	08.00 to 16.00 or 16.30

Bank hours

Monday to Friday	09.30 to 16.00
Thursday	09.30 to 18.00

Vat rate	Standard: 22%

Types of Business Entity

Public limited company – *Aktieselskab (AS)*
A public limited company requires a minimum capital of Kr 300,000. The company must maintain a list of shareholders who own shares carrying at least 10 per cent of the voting rights or representing at least 10 per cent of the share capital (but not less than Kr 100,000). Management is vested in a board of directors to be composed of not less than three members. If the company is listed on the stock exchange, the disclosure requirements are very extensive.

Private limited company – *Anpartsselskab (APS)*
A private limited company is subject to fewer formalities than a public limited company in several respects. The capital requirement is a minimum Kr 80,000, and there is no maximum. The majority of Danish limited liability companies are private limited companies.

Partnership
   General – *Interessentskab (IS)*
   A business association of two or more partners (individuals or corporate bodies) with joint and several liability.
   Limited – *Kommanditselskab (KS)*
   A business association of one or more general partners (individuals or corporate bodies) having joint and several liability, with one or more limited partners (individuals or corporate bodies) having liability up to a certain amount.

Branch office
A foreign joint stock company which is duly incorporated in its home country may carry on business activities in Denmark through a registered branch office.

Co-operative societies – *Andelsselskaber*
A co-operative society is a corporate body formed for the purpose of processing and selling members' products or for the purpose of purchasing goods for sale to members.

Sole proprietorship – *Enkeltmandsfirma*
A sole proprietorship may be registered in the Register of Business Names in order to protect the style of the firm.

The principal purpose of an APS is to make it easy for the establishment of small companies with limited liability and is similar to the GmbH of Germany and the French SARL. The APS is the business entity we shall cover in this chapter.

As a general rule, no authorisation is required for setting up business entities in Denmark. This means, that in principle all business entities imaginable can be used. However, authorisation is necessary for the private limited company (APS). The necessary forms for authorisation are available at the Danish Commerce and Companies Agency. The forms are not available in English and the Agency does not otherwise publish information in any foreign language.

It may take up to 6 months to register a company at the Registrar of Companies. An unregistered company cannot acquire rights nor incur obligations. However, the company may commence operations from the date of the formation agreement, but on the joint responsibility of the promoters, the members of the board of directors and management.

It has become customary to acquire the shares in an already registered company which has not carried out any business. Subsequently, the necessary adjustments are made to the bylaws in order to conform to the situation in question, i.e. adjustments concerning name, purpose, increase of capital, the election of a new board of directors and accountants.

The company can be acquired via the lawyers who incorporated the company for an amount which includes the registration fee, the capital investment tax, costs incurred by the lawyer and a fee to the latter.

An AS may be bought at approximately Kr 307,000 and an APS at approximately Kr 83,000.

Formation Procedures – APS

A formation agreement (*stiftelsesoverenskomst*) must be drawn up and signed by the promoters. The following information must be included in the agreement:

- the name and addresses of the promoters (one or more), directors and accountants
- the bylaws (*vedtaegter*)
- the shares subscribed for by the promoters
- the price at which shares are offered for subscription and the deadline for the payment
- whether the company is to pay the cost in connection with the formation; if the latter is the case, information on the stipulated costs
- if the promoters or others have special rights, an outline on this
- the contents of any agreement which imposes a substantial economic obligation on the company

The bylaws must include the following:

- the name of the company
- the residence of the company
- the purpose of the company
- the size of the share capital (minimum Kr 80,000)
- whether the share capital is held by more than one shareholder; if the latter is the case, the size of the shares subscribed for and the shareholders' voting rights
- whether there will be a board of directors (only required if the registered capital is at least Kr 300,000)
  Note: If the APS has no board of directors, then the duties normally performed by the board of directors must be carried out by the General Manager
- numbers of accountants. (It is not necessary to give details of their names and addresses.)
- when and where the general meeting will take place
- agenda for the general meeting
- accounting period
- if the shares are not freely transferable, the restriction must be included in the bylaws. The same will apply if the com-

pany has a right to redeem the shares or there is restriction in the director's possibility of signing for the company.

Application for registration at the Register of Companies (*Erhvervs og Selskabsstyrelsen*) must be made no later than 2 months after the date of the formation agreement. A special form which can be obtained at the Register of Companies must be used and the formation agreement as well as the bylaws must be enclosed. The application must be in Danish; if the formation agreement and the bylaws are in English, an authorised translation must be enclosed as well.

The name of the company must be distinctive. It must clearly differ from the names of other private limited companies as well as public limited companies. No family name, company name, special name on real estate, trademark, trade characteristics etc. must be included in the name, if it belongs to others. However, when choosing your business name (in your own language) ensure that it would not be offensive when translated into Danish.

The formation documents are published in the Official Gazette (*Statstidende*) by the Registrar of Companies. The documents are open to public inspection, and copies may be obtained from the Registrar of Companies. Once the formation procedure is completed, the company will get a registration number and a certification of the information registered.

An APS registered company needs to notify the tax authorities and the employer control in the region where the APS company is located. Technically, it is possible to complete the formation yourself.

Formation Costs

The registration fee is Kr 1,700 plus 0.4 per cent of the nominal value of the share capital. Furthermore, a capital investment tax of 1 per cent of the nominal value of the share capital will be payable. In addition, there will be fees to lawyers and accountants.

Assuming a minimum capital of 80,000:

Registration fee	Kr 1700
0.4% of share capital	Kr 320
Capital Investment Tax of share capital – 1%	Kr 800
Fees to lawyers, printing etc	Kr 2000
Approximate total cost	Kr 4820

General

It is also worth noting the following:

- Founders need not be citizens of Denmark or residents.
- If an APS loses more than half of its share capital then it must be re-capitalised.
- An APS does not issue share certificates.
- However, membership certificates may be issued. These must be registered in the name of the holders and are non-negotiable.
- An APS must be listed with the Danish Commerce and Company Agency.
- An APS (like all other forms of business enterprise) must file financial statements which include: balance sheet, profit and loss account and annual report. These must be sent to the Danish Commerce and Company Agency not more than one month after the accounts have been approved, and not more than seven months after the close of the accounting year.

Useful Vocabulary

Aliens Department	Direktoratet for Udlaendinge
Bank Inspectorate	Finanstilsynet
Board of Directors	Bestyrelsen
Board of Management	Direktion
Bylaws	Vedtaegter
Capital Investment Tax	Kapitaltilforselsafgift
Companies Act 1973	Anpartsselskabsloven
Danish Official Gazette	Statstidende
Formation agreement	Stiftelsesoverenskomst
Health and Safety at Work Act	
	Arbejdsmiloloven
Inland Revenue Department	
	Skattedepartementet
Inland Revenue directorate	
	Statsskattedirektoratet
Institute of state authorised public accountants	
	Foreningen af Statsautoriserede Revisorer
Labour exchange	Arbejdsformidlingen
National Tax Tribunal	Landsskatteretten
Payment in kind	Apportindskud
Public Corporations Act	Aktieselskabsloven
Register of Companies	Erhvervs og Selskabsstyrelsen
Registered public accountant	Registreret revisor
Security Registration	Vaedipapircentralen
Share Transfer Tax Act	Aktieafgiftsloven
Society of registered public accountants	Foreningen af Registrerede Revisorer
State authorised public accountant	Statsautoriseret revisor
Statutory meeting	Konstituerende generalforsamling
Tax Assessment Council	Ligningsradet
Value Added Tax	Mervaediafgift/MOMS
Workers Protection Act	Arbejdsbeskyttelsesloven

11

IRELAND

Population	3 million
Capital city	Dublin
Largest cities (by population)	Cork Limerick Galway Waterford
Currency	Irish Pound

Main holidays – 1992

New Year's Day	1 Jan
St Patrick's Day	17 Mar
Good Friday	17 Apr
Easter Monday	20 Apr
Bank Holiday	1 June
Bank Holiday	3 Aug
Bank Holiday	26 Oct
Christmas Day	25 Dec
St. Stephen's Day	26 Dec

Business working days	Monday to Friday
Business hours	09.30 to 17.30
Bank hours	10.00 to 12.30 13.30 to 15.00
Vat rate	Low: 10% Standard: 23%

Types of Business Entity

Public limited company (PLC)
These are companies with limited liability, but detailed registration and disclosure requirements apply. The minimum share capital is IR £30,000 of which at least 25 per cent must be paid up. The minimum number of shareholders is seven and there is no maximum. Shares must have a par value.

Private limited company (LTD)
Private limited companies have limited liability, a minimum of 2 and a maximum of 50 shareholders, and less onerous disclosure requirements than a public limited company.

Partnerships
Partnerships do not have a separate legal personality and are usually formed by a partnership deed, which sets out the full conditions under which the partnership will operate. No specific capital structure is laid down by law.

Joint ventures
There are arrangements between parties to participate together in an enterprise, in a manner set out in an agreement between them. They do not necessarily involve the establishment of a separate legal entity.

Branch of a foreign company
Branches of foreign companies carry the legal personality of the foreign parent and are not recognised in Irish law as an entity separate from the company of which they form a part.

Sole proprietor
This form of enterprise involves an individual engaging in trade, receiving all the profits and incurring all the liabilities of that trade.

[121]

Company Incorporation Procedures

Private limited companies are the most common form of company registered in Ireland. There are currently 105,812 companies registered and 14,541 companies were formed in 1989. It is this type of company that we deal with in this chapter.

Any two or more persons, associated for a lawful purpose can, by subscribing their names to a Memorandum of Association and complying with the requirements of the Companies Acts, form a private limited company.

Company names

In addition to complying with the procedures for registration, applicants must also satisfy themselves in advance of the acceptability of the proposed company name.

Since the Registrar of Companies does not give provisional name approval, it is important that persons forming companies should satisfy themselves in advance of the acceptability of the proposed name, bearing in mind that an objection might be received which could result in the company being directed to change its name.

Generally speaking, a name will not be registered if:

- it is identical to a name already appearing on the register of companies
- in the opinion of the Minister it is offensive
- it would suggest State sponsorship

Where to check

Applicants are advised to check whether the name proposed is the same as one already registered by checking the register of companies, i.e. microfiche and also the computer printout for those later names not yet on the microfiche. These can be checked free of charge at the Companies Office. Persons who are not in a position to check names in the Companies Office may purchase the microfiche and place a request for an update at regular intervals.

How to check

In determining the similarity of names, certain words and their abbreviations together with accents and punctuation marks will be ignored. These words include the definite article and the words 'company', 'co', and '&', 'service', 'services', 'limited', etc. Names which are phonetically identical but not visually identical will be allowed.

If a name includes words which imply specific functions, e.g. 'Holding Company' or 'Group', further information may be required to support the application.

Prohibitions and restrictions

Names containing certain words cannot be used unless approved by relevant bodies. For example, the words 'Bank, 'Banker', 'Banking', may only be used with the permission of the Central Bank. This applies to names such as 'Hollybank', 'Sweetbank', 'Canal Bank', etc., and the surname 'Banks' even though the company may not intend to carry on banking business. The following words cannot be used: 'Society', 'Co-op', 'Co-operative', 'Insurance'.

Note:

The following matters are prohibited by law:

- Banking objects are not permitted unless a license has been obtained from the Central Bank of Ireland.
- A company is excluded from holding a bookmaker's license under the Betting Acts 1926–1931.
- A company cannot act as auditor, receiver or liquidator for another company.
- It is not permitted to carry on the business of Insurance unless the Insurance Acts have been complied with.
- A credit union, trade union or building society cannot be incorporated as a limited company.
- Broadcasting is prohibited, unless the permission of the Minister for Communications has been obtained.

Direction to change a company name

When an objection to a name being 'identical to' or 'too like' another already registered is received, the complainant will be asked to submit his reasons and any available evidence of confusion which may have arisen.

Formation Procedures

Incorporation of private limited company
The following documents are required:

- Memorandum and Articles of Association
- Form A1

The Memorandum and Articles must be typed or printed. The form of the memorandum is set out in Table B of the Companies Act. (It should comply with the Companies Acts 1963–1986 and be printed in clear black print on durable paper.) It must be divided into paragraphs and numbered consecutively. A margin of 1.5 inches should be left on the left-hand side to allow for binding into the Companies Office file.

The memorandum must contain the following particulars:
- the name of the company with limited or *teoranta* as the last word of the name
- the objects of the company
- it must state that the liability of the members is limited
- it must also indicate the amount of share capital to be registered and the division thereof into shares of a fixed amount
- no subscriber of the Memorandum may take less than one share.

The Memorandum must be signed by at least 2 subscribers. The subscribers should sign the memorandum in their own handwriting, photocopied signatures will not suffice. Their residential address should be given and the number of shares should be written in full in their own handwriting, e.g. 'one share'. Their signatures must be witnessed and dated.

The Articles must be divided into paragraphs and numbered consecutively. They must be signed by the subscribers, their addresses and descriptions must be stated and their signatures must be witnessed and dated.

The full name of the company should be given in the memorandum and articles, the abbreviation 'Ltd' is not acceptable and the correct statutes e.g. 'Companies Acts 1963 to 1986' should also be cited.

Regulation for the Management of a Private Company Limited by Shares are set out in Table A, Part 11 of the Companies Act. If it is intended to form a company without registering separate Articles, the applicant for registration should submit a document stating that the company wishes to adopt as its Articles Part 11 of Table A.

Form A1:

- The name of the company should be given in full on the form.
- The registered office of the company must be in the State. P.O. Box numbers are not acceptable.
- At least two directors and one secretary must sign the form. If the articles state a commencement number of directors or name the directors/secretary, the number and name on the form A1 must coincide.
- All first names of directors and secretary must be shown; initials are not acceptable.
- The business occupation and other directorships in the State must be completed.
- Residential addresses of directors and secretary must be given.
- Each director and secretary must sign his/her consent on the form and date it.
- If the form is signed by an agent for the subscribers, it should be signed and dated by an individual for each subscriber; a company name will not suffice.
- The declaration of compliance must be properly sworn and must be dated on or after the dates given on the memorandum and articles and form A1. Otherwise it will have to be redeclared. *Note* – The declaration of compliance, must be completed by either a solicitor engaged in the formation of the company or a person named as Director or Secretary of the company.

- Companies' capital duty statement should be completed in full.
- The nominal capital and issued capital must coincide with that given in the Memorandum and Articles of Association.
- Any amendments made to the Memorandum and Articles of form A1 should be initialled.

Capital
The minimum share capital is £100 and there is no upper limit. Subscribers need only take up one share each (minimum two) of £1 each.

Formation Expenses

Registration fee	£116
Capital duty*	£1
General duty and filing fees	£25

* Capital duty is charged at the rate of 1% on subscribed capital (minimum of £1).

Obligation to Show Certain Information

The following particulars must be exhibited conspicuously at every place of business in the State:

- the name of the company
- the name of the country in which the company is incorporated
- if applicable, the fact that the liability of the members of the company is limited

The following particulars must be stated in legible characters on all company bill heads, letter paper, notices, etc:

- the name of the company
- the name of the country in which the company is incorporated (if applicable), the fact that the liability of the

members of the company is limited, and in respect of each director, the following details:
present Christian name, or the initials thereof, and present surname; any former Christian names and surnames; and nationality, if not Irish.

If the company commenced to trade under a name other than its corporate name, the Business Name must be registered under the Registration of Business Names Act, 1963 on Form RBN1C.

Search Fees (includes fees for computer-based services)

Manual company file search	£2.00
Manual business name file search	£2.00
Company file search by post	£6.00
Business name file search by post	£5.00
Company printout*	£1.50
Business name printout*	£1.50
Telex enquiry partial search by return	£2.00
full search at end of day	£4.00
full search by return	£6.00

* By post, there is an additional charge of £1.00 postage and handling, irrespective of the number of companies/business names searched.

Forms
These are available from Companies House (see useful addresses).

12

LUXEMBOURG

Population	0.5 million
Capital city	Luxembourg
Largest cities (by population)	Esch-Sur-Alzette Ettelbruck
Currency	Luxembourg Franc (F.lux)

Main holidays – 1992

New Year's Day	1 Jan
Easter Monday	20 Apr
May Day	1 May
Ascension Day	28 May
Whit Monday	8 June
National Day	23 June
Assumption	15 Aug
All Saints' Day	1 Nov
Christmas Day	25 Dec
St. Stephen's Day	26 Dec

Business working days	Monday to Friday
Business hours	08.00 to 12.00 14.00 to 18.00
Bank hours	09.00 to 12.00 13.00 to 16.30
Vat rate	Low: 3–6% Standard: 12%

Types of Business Entity

Joint stock company, public company or corporation – *Société Anonyme (SA)*
A joint stock compay is similar to the UK public limited company. Its members put up only a given amount and the company's capital is divided into freely transferable shares.

It must be formed by deed prepared by a notary and published in full. There must be at least two shareholders, the capital must be fully subscribed and at least 25 per cent paid up.

Limited liability company – *Société à Responsibilité Limité (SARL)*
In the SARL the number of shareholders is limited by law and they cannot put up more than a given amount. Their shares can be transferred only as provided for by law. It must be formed by deed prepared by notary and published in full. The number of shareholders must be neither less than 2 or more than 40. The capital of the company must amount to not less than F.lux 500,000 fully subscribed and paid up. The Company is managed by one or more managers, who need not be members. The holding of an annual general meeting is not compulsory, if the number of members is not above 25. No internal governing body is prescribed. In larger companies, external auditors are entrusted with the supervision. The company cannot raise a loan by public issue of bonds or make a public issue of shares. The company is subject to corporation tax.

General partnership – *Société en nom Collectif (SENC)*
A general partnership is formed under a business name by two or more persons, all of whom are personally, jointly and severally and indefinitely liable for the company's debts.

Limited partnership – *Société en Commandite Simple (SECS)*
A limited partnership is formed under a business name by one or more partners ('general partners') who are jointly and severally and indefinitely liable, and one or more 'limited partners' who merely contribute capital and are liable only to the extent of their contribution.

[131]

There is a combined form of Limited Liability company and Limited partnership (SARL & CIE, SECS), which combines the principles of both patterns. This variant, which is derived from German law, has the advantage of limiting the liability of the general partner and at the same time avoiding the company being taxed in its own capacity as an entity separate from its members.

Partnership limited by shares – *Société en Commandite par Actions (SECA)*
The partnership limited by shares is similar to the partnership with limited liability (*société en commandite simple*), the only difference being that the holdings of the limited partners consist of freely transferable shares. Supervision must be entrusted to one or more auditors.

Joint venture – *Association Momentanée*
The purpose of an *association momentanée* (joint venture) is to carry out one or more specified commercial operations without trading under a name. It does not acquire legal personality. Its members are jointly and severally liable to third parties with whom they have dealt.

Holding companies
A holding company does not constitute a special form of company but is it an ordinary company formed for a specific purpose. As a rule holding companies take the status of *Société Anonyme*. It is not, however, permitted to engage in trade or industry on its own account.

The branch of a foreign enterprise
A foreign company wishing to establish a branch in the Grand Duchy must publish its act of incorporation beforehand in the Grand Duchy.
The word 'branch' means any subsidiary unit, dependent commercial centre or any base of operations whatever, which is well and truly established in a fixed location and where a

resident employee represents the company and deals with the public on its behalf.'

Co-operative society – *Société Cooperative*
The co-operative society has no prescribed name and is composed of members whose number and holdings vary and whose shares are not transferable to third parties.

Non-commercial company – *Société Civile*
The *Société Civile* is subject to the provisions of Article 1982 et seq. of the Civil Code and can be formed by deed under private seal published in full in the Official Gazette.

It has a legal personality of its own and can be changed into a commercial company by decision of a general meeting specially convened for the purpose. This type of company is especially suitable for partnerships in the liberal professions.

Legislation

The company that we will be looking at in this chapter is the SARL.

In the Grand Duchy of Luxembourg, company law is based on the Law of 10 August 1915 as amended mainly by the Law of 18 September 1933 on the establishment of a limited liability company (*Société à responsabilité limitée*), the Law of 23 November 1972 on the adaption to the Law of 1915 to Directive No 68/51 of the Council of the European Communities of 9 March 1968 and the Law of 4 May 1984 with the provisions of the Fourth EC Directive for corporations.

Luxembourg legislation in this field is largely based on the Belgian Law of 1913 on the same subject. On any questions of interpretation, therefore, reference must be made to Belgian case-law and commentaries.

Formation Procedures

The incorporation of a SARL is achieved by a notarial deed of incorporation which requires a few formalities. Documents required are:

- complete set of articles of incorporation (called statutes) for the notarial deed to be prepared
- a bank certificate (or auditor's certificate for payment in kind)
- a proxy for the founders not appearing personally before the notary at the deed to incorporation

The first and third can be prepared by the notary, but the second must be issued by the bank where the cash contribution is deposited and will act as evidence of receipt of the share capital. This must then be sent to the notary.

The articles of incorporation may be in any language. If they are in a language other than French or German, they must be followed by a translation into French or German.

Articles of Incorporation

The Articles of Incorporation (*Acte de Constitution*) is compulsory and has to be prepared with an authorised notary; it has to be registered and deposited with the *Greffe* of the *Tribunal de Commerce*.

The articles must include:

- identity of the natural or legal persons by, or on behalf of whom, it has been signed
- form of the corporation and its name
- registered office
- objects of the corporation
- amount of the subscribed capital and, where applicable, the authorised capital
- amount of the initial subscribed capital contribution paid up
- details of the different classes of shares, the rights attached to each class and the number of shares subscribed; in the case of authorised capital, the amount of each class of shares to be issued and the rights attached to each class

- whether the shares are bearer or registered; joint share-holders are not allowed
- details of any contributions to capital made other than in cash and the conditions under which they are made, including the name of contributor and the report of the independent auditor (*reviseur d'entreprises*)
- the extent of any advantages given to the founder share-holders at the time of constitution and the reason(s) for granting the advantages
- if applicable, arrangements for particular voting rights that do not represent stated capital
- in so far as they are not provided by law, the rules for determining the number and basis of selection of members of the board of directors, management and auditors, and their responsibilities
- life of the corporation
- amount (at least an estimate) of the cost of incorporation

The following fees are payable:

- 1 per cent registration duties (minimum F.lux 500,000 × 1% = F.lux 5,000) of issued capital
- Notarial fees including lodging and publishing in the official gazette (approx. F.lux 40,000)
- If incorporation through a lawyer's office or an international fiduciary company, formation fees about F.lux 60,000

The name of the company must be different from that of any other company already existing in Luxembourg. Clearance for the proposed name is obtained from the Register of Commerce through the notary, the lawyer, or the fiduciary company.

The founders receive the notarised articles (one original for each) and 2 months later an extract from the Register of Companies. The notarised articles will be published in the office gazette (Memorial) in Luxembourg and will be available to the general public at the Register of Commerce.

In each district a Trade and Companies Register (*Registre de Commerce et des Sociétés*) is kept at the Commercial Court. A new SARL must register and provide the following information:

- type and object of the company

- exact address of the registered offices
- the share capital
- names of the shareholders
- names of the persons who are entitled to represent the company

The Fourth Directive

The Fourth EC Directive was introduced in Luxembourg with the Law of 4 May 1984 (Official Gazette A No. 4 of 10 May 1984). Prior to this date a SARL was not required to publish its financial statements, unless it was a credit establishment. However, publication documents for the SARL are now governed by the fourth directive.

Compliance with requirements of the law is required if any two of the three following criteria are fulfilled:

	Large companies F.lux Millions	Medium companies F.lux Millions	Small companies F.lux Millions
Total balance sheet	310	310	77
Net turnover	640	640	160
Number of employees (average)	250	250	50

For all companies, a balance sheet, profit and loss account and notes to accounts have to be prepared, together with a financial report and (for medium and large companies) an auditors' opinion. Small companies may publish just the balance sheet and abridged notes to accounts. As a general rule, publication is achieved by a mention in the Official Gazette that the deposit of the documents at the *Greffe du Tribunal* has been made.

The financial report need not be published but has to be kept available for inspection at the registered office.

Capital
- A SARL may reduce its capital.

[136]

- A SARL must establish a legal reserve.
- A SARL may not issue bonds or make a public issue of shares.
- Capital must be wholly issued and fully paid up on formation.

Shares and Shareholders

- Shares are non-negotiable.
- Shares are transferable only on 75 per cent agreement of shareholders.
- Share transfers are by notarial deed.
- Shares must be denominated in Luxembourg francs, with a minimum value of F.lux 1000.
- Shares must be in registered form. They are not freely negotiable and may be transferred only with the agreement of holders of at least 75 per cent of the share capital. The transfer is required to be effected by notarial deed and accordingly must be published in the official gazette.
- A SARL may acquire its own shares although only out of profits and free reserves.
- An annual general meeting of shareholders is not required if the number of members is less than 25.

General

- A SARL may exist for an unlimited period of time.
- The management may rest with one person (the *gérant*).
- A statutory auditor need not be appointed for a SARL if the company has fewer than twenty-five members.
- In addition to legally required accounting records, a SARL must maintain a register containing the company's original articles and any subsequent change thereto; and the name, profession and residence of each shareholder together with details of shareholdings.
- Formation requires at least two founder shareholders, and a

minimum fully subscribed and paid in capital of F.lux 500,000.

- Every entity engaged in business activity must within one month from commencement of business apply to be entered in the trade register kept in Luxembourg and Diekirch district courts.

Notes: Draft law foresees that there can be a minimum of one and up to 40 shareholders.

A company must disclose its full name, legal status, the address of its registered office, the name of the Commercial Court of registration as well as the registration number and paid-up capital, on all business stationery including deeds, notices, publications, letterheads and invoices.

The company must register with the local VAT office within 15 days of commencing activities.

Useful Vocabulary

Bankings and savings institutions	Etablissements bancaires et d'épargne
Belgo-Luxembourge economic union (BLEU)	Union économique belgo-luxembourgeoise (UEBL)
Chamber of Commerce	Chambre de Commerce
Commercial Court	Tribunal de Commerce
Commercial register	Registre aux Firms
Companies annual tax	Taxe d'abonnement
Corporate income tax	Impôt sur le revenue des collectivies/Korperschaftsteur
Corporation tax	Impôt sur le revenu des conectivities
Department of registration and properties	l'Administration de l'enregistrement et des domaines
External auditors	Reviseur d'entreprise
Managers	Gérants
Minister of Labour	Ministre du Travail
Ministry for small and medium sized firms and trades	Ministère des Classes Moyennes
Municipal business tax	Impôt commercial communal/Gewerbesteuer
Official gazette	Memorial
Ordinary shares	Actions de capital ordinaires
Personal income tax	Impôt sur le revenu des personnes physiques
Preferred stock	Actions de capital privilegées
Property tax	Impôt sur le patrimoine
Public employment offices	Bureaux de placement publics
Registration taxes	Droits d'enregistrement
Rural banks	Caisses rurales
Shares without voting rights	Actions sans droit de vote
State savings bank	Caisse d'Epargne de l'Etat
Statutes	Acte de Constitution
Statutory auditor	Commissaire aux comptes
Tax collection office	Administration des Contribution
Tax on land and buildings	Impôt foncier
Value Added Tax	Taxe sur la valeur ajoutée

Appendix I

UNITED KINGDOM: SPECIMEN DOCUMENTS

Please note: Objects of the Company – This section has been designed to give you broad clauses that cover almost every conceivable business enterprise.

COMPANIES ACT 1985
PRIVATE COMPANY LIMITED BY SHARES
MEMORANDUM OF ASSOCIATION

1. The company's name is (name of your company) Limited.
2. The company's registered office shall be situated in England and Wales.
3. The company's objects are:
   a) To carry on all or any business of:
   i) financiers and capitalists
   ii) an investment company in all its branches
   iii) providing brokerage, consultancy and agency services of any nature
   iv) developing or dealing in property or any interest therein
   v) manufacturing, funding, leasing, refining, installations, packaging, publishing, distributing, selling, marketing, wholesaling, retailing, discounting, exporting, importing, storing, shipping, hiring, franchising, or otherwise trading or investing in merchandise of any description or any interest therein.
   vi) any other business which, in the opinion of the Directors can be advantageously carried on in connection with or ancillary to the business of the company.
   b) To borrow monies whether secured or not and to do all other things which may be deemed incidental or conducive to the attainment of any of the company's objects.
   c) To distribute amongst the members of a company any monies or other property of the company of whatever nature.
4. None of the objects of the company shall be narrowly construed or given precedence over any other object.

5. The liability of the members is limited.
6. The company's share capital is —— shares of —— pounds each.

WITNESSED SIGNATURE OF SUBSCRIBERS
We, the several persons whose Names, Addresses and Descriptions are subscribed, are desirous of being formed into a Company, in pursuance of this Memorandum of Association, and we respectively agree to take the number of Shares in the Capital of the Company set opposite our respective names.

NAMES, ADDRESSES AND DESCRIPTIONS OF SUBSCRIBERS	Number of shares taken by each Subscriber
NEIL HOLLIS 13 VILLA ROAD BIRMINGHAM Signature of above Bookseller	ONE
JULIE PEARCE 2 ALBERT ROAD TAMWORTH Signature of above Sales Clerk	ONE

Dated   day of   19
Witness to the above Signatures:
Jane Hollis's signature   JANE HOLLIS
                                 13 VILLA ROAD
                                 BIRMINGHAM
                                 Housewife

APPENDIX I

THE COMPANIES ACT 1985

COMPANY LIMITED BY SHARES

ARTICLES OF ASSOCIATION
of

1. Subject as hereinafter provided, the regulations contained in Table A in The Companies (Tables A to F) Regulations 1985 (hereinafter referred to as 'Table A') shall apply to the Company.

2. Regulations 8, 64, 76, 77 and 113 of Table A shall not apply to the Company.

3. The Company is a private company and accordingly no offer or invitation shall be made to the public (whether for cash or otherwise) to subscribe for any shares in or debentures of the Company, nor shall the Company allot or agree to allot (whether for cash or otherwise) any shares in or debentures of the Company with a view to all or any of those shares or debentures being offered for sale to the public.

4. At the date of the adoption of these Articles the capital of the Company is £100 divided into 100 Ordinary Shares of £1 each.

5. a) The Directors may submit to Article 6 hereof allot, grant options over, or otherwise deal with or dispose of any relevant securities (as defined by section 80(2) of the Companies Act 1985) of the Company to such persons and generally on such terms and conditions as the Directors think proper.

   b) The general authority conferred by paragraph (a) of this Article shall be conditional upon due compliance with Article 6 hereof and shall extend to the amount of the authorised share capital of the Company upon its incorporation. The said authority will expire on   19   unless renewed, varied or revoked by the Company in general meeting in accordance with the said section 80.

   c) The Directors shall be entitled under the general authority conferred by paragraph (a) of this Article to make at any time before the expiry of such authority any offer or agreement which will or might require relevant securities of the Company to be allotted after the expiry of such authority.

6. a) Subject to any direction to the contrary that may be given by the Company in general meeting all shares authorised pursuant to Article 5 hereof to be allotted shall be offered to the members in proportion to the existing shares held by them and such offer shall be made by notice in writing specifying the number of the shares to which the member is entitled and limiting a time (being no less than 21 days) within which the offer if not accepted will be deemed to have been declined, and after the expiry of such time or upon receipt of an intimation from the member to whom such notice is given that he declines to accept the shares offered, the Directors

[143]

may, subject to these Articles, allot or otherwise dispose of the same to such persons and upon such terms as they think most beneficial to the Company. The Directors may in like manner dispose of any such shares as aforesaid which, by reason of the proportion borne by them to the number of persons entitled to any such offer as aforesaid or by reason of any other difficulty in apportioning the same, cannot in the opinion of the Directors be conveniently offered in manner hereinbefore provided.

b) By virtue of section 91(1) of the Companies Act 1985, sections 89(1) and 90(1) to 90(6) inclusive of that Act shall not apply to the Company.

7. The Company shall have a first and paramount lien on every share (whether or not it is a fully paid share) for all monies (whether presently payable or not) called or payable at a fixed time in respect of that share and the Company shall also have a first and paramount lien on all shares (whether fully paid or not) standing registered in the name of any member whether solely or one of two or more joint holders for all monies presently payable by him or his estate to the Company; but the Directors may at any time declare any share to be wholly or in part exempt from the provisions of this Article. The Company's lien (if any) on a share shall extend to all dividends payable thereon.

8. The Directors may, in their absolute discretion and without assigning any reason therefore, decline to register any transfer of any share, whether or not it is a fully paid share. The first sentence of regulation 24 of Table A shall not apply to the Company.

9. In accordance with section 372(3) of the Companies Act 1985 in every notice calling a General Meeting of the Company there shall appear with reasonable prominence a statement that a member entitled to attend and vote is entitled to appoint a proxy to attend and vote instead of him and that a proxy need not be a member of the Company. Regulation 38 of Table A shall be modified accordingly and the second sentence of Regulation 59 of Table A shall not apply to the Company.

10. In Regulation 41 of Table A there shall be added at the end: 'If at any adjourned meeting a quorum is not present within half an hour from the time appointed for the meeting, the meeting shall be dissolved'.

11. Unless and until the Company in general meeting shall otherwise determine, there shall be no maximum number of Directors and the minimum number of Directors shall be one. If and so long as there is a sole Director he may exercise all the powers and authorities vested in the Directors by these Articles and by Table A and Regulation 89 of Table A shall be modified accordingly. The first Directors of the Company shall be named in the statement delivered to the Registrar of Companies pursuant to section 10 of the Companies Act 1985.

12. The Company shall not be subject to section 293 of the Companies Act 1985, and accordingly any person may be appointed or elected as a Director, whatever his age, and no Director shall be required to vacate his office of Director by reason of his attaining or having attained the age of seventy years or any other age.

13.   No person other than a Director retiring by rotation shall be elected a Director at any general meeting unless—

i)   he is recommended by the Directors; or

ii)   not less than fourteen or more than thirty-five clear days before the date of the meeting a notice in writing signed by a member qualified to vote at the meeting has been given to the Company of the intention of propose that person for election, together with a notice in writing signed by that person of his willingness to be elected.

14.   A director shall not be required to hold any share qualification but shall nevertheless be entitled to receive notice of and to attend at all general meetings of the Company and at all separate general meetings of the holders of any class of shares in the capital of the Company.

NAMES, ADDRESSES AND DESCRIPTIONS OF SUBSCRIBERS

NEIL HOLLIS
13 VILLA ROAD
BIRMINGHAM
   Signature of above
Bookseller

JULIE PEARCE
2 ALBERT ROAD
TAMWORTH
   Signature of above
Sales Clerk

Dated the   day of 19
Witness to the above Signatures:
JANE HOLLIS
13 VILLA ROAD
BIRMINGHAM
   Signature of Jane Hollis
Housewife

TABLE A
   This can be found in the 1985 Companies Act book which can be obtained from Her Majesty's Stationery Offices (HMSO).

COMPANIES FORM No. 10

Statement of first directors and secretary and intended situation of registered office

10

Pursuant to section 10 of the Companies Act 1985

To the Registrar of Companies
(Address overleaf - Note 8)

For official use

Name of company

*

The intended situation of the registered office of the company on incorporation is as stated below

Postcode

If the memorandum is delivered by an agent for the subscribers of the memorandum please mark 'X'in the box opposite and insert the agent's name and address below

Postcode

Number of continuation sheets attached (see note 1)

Presentor's name address and reference (if any):

For official Use
General Section

Post room

Page 1

[146]

APPENDIX I

The name(s) and particulars of the person who is, or the persons who are, to be the first director or directors of the company (note 2) are as follows:

Name (note 3)	Business occupation
Previous name(s) (note 3)	Nationality
Address (note 4)	
Postcode	Date of birth (where applicable) (note 6)
Other directorships †	
I consent to act as director of the company named on page 1	
Signature	Date

Name (note 3)	Business occupation
Previous name(s) (note 3)	Nationality
Address (note 4)	
Postcode	Date of birth (where applicable) (note 6)
Other directorships †	
I consent to act as director of the company named on page 1	
Signature	Date

Name (note 3)	Business occupation
Previous name(s) (note 3)	Nationality
Address (note 4)	
Postcode	Date of birth (where applicable) (note 6)
Other directorships †	
I consent to act as director of the company named on page 1	
Signature	Date

[147]

The name(s) and particulars of the person who is, or the persons who are, to be the first secretary, or joint secretaries, of the company are as follows:

Name (notes 3 & 7)	
Previous name(s) (note 3)	
Address (notes 4 & 7)	
	Postcode
I consent to act as secretary of the company named on page 1	
Signature	Date

Name (notes 3 & 7)	
Previous name(s) (note 3)	
Address (notes 4 & 7)	
	Postcode
I consent to act as secretary of the company named on page 1	
Signature	Date

Signature of agent on behalf of subscribers	Date

Signed	Date
Signed	Date
Signed	Date
Signed	Date
Signed	Date
Signed	Date

Page 3

[148]

Notes

1 If the spaces on Page 2 are insufficient the names and particulars must be entered on the prescribed continuation sheet(s).

2 'Director' includes any person who occupies the position of a director, by whatever name called.

3. For an individual, his present christian name(s) and surname must be given, together with any previous christian name(s) or surname(s).

"Christian name" includes a forename. In the case of a peer or person usually known by a title different from his surname, "surname" means that title. In the case of a corporation, its corporate name must be given.

A previous christian name or surname need not be given if:—

(a) in the case of a married woman, it was a name by which she was known before her marriage; or

(b) it was changed or ceased to be used at least 20 years ago, or before the person who previously used it reached the age of 18; or

(c) in the case of a peer or a person usually known by a British title different from his surname, it was a name by which he was known before he adopted the title or succeeded to it

4 Usual residential address must be given or, in the case of a corporation, the registered or principal office.

5 The names must be given of all bodies corporate incorporated in Great Britain of which the director is also a director, or has been a director at any time during the preceeding five years.

However, a present or past directorship need not be disclosed if it is, or has been, held in a body corporate which, throughout that directorship, has been:—

(a) a dormant company (which is a company which has had no transactions required to be entered in the company's accounting records, except any which may have arisen from the taking of shares in the company by a subscriber to the memorandum as such).

(b) a body corporate of which the company making the return was a wholly-owned subsidiary;

(c) a wholly-owned subsidiary of the company making the return; or

(d) a wholly-owned subsidiary of a body corporate of which the company making the return was also a wholly owned subsidiary.

6. Dates of birth need only be given if the company making the return is:—

(a) a public company;
(b) the subsidiary of a public company; or
(c) the subsidiary of a public company registered in Northern Ireland

7 Where all the partners in a firm are joint secretaries, only the name and principal office of the firm need be stated.

Where the secretary or one of the joint secretaries is a Scottish firm the details required are the firm name and its principal office.

8 The address for companies registered in England and Wales or Wales is:-

The Registrar of Companies
Companies House
Crown Way
Cardiff
CF4 3UZ

or, for companies registered in Scotland:-

The Registrar of Companies
Companies House
100-102 George Street
Edinburgh
EH2 3DJ

COMPANIES FORM No. 12

**Statutory Declaration of compliance
with requirements on application
for registration of a company**

12

Please do not
write in
this margin

Pursuant to section 12(3) of the Companies Act 1985

Please complete,
legibly, preferably
in black type, or
bold block lettering

To the Registrar of Companies
(Address overleaf)

For official use   For official use

Name of company

* insert full
name of Company

I, _____

of _____

_____

_____

† delete as
appropriate

do solemnly and sincerely declare that I am a [Solicitor engaged in the formation of the company]†
[person named as director or secretary of the company in the statement delivered to the registrar
under section 10(2)]† and that all the requirements of the above Act in respect of the registration of the
above company and of matters precedent and incidental to it have been complied with,

And I make this solemn declaration conscientiously believing the same to be true and by virtue of the

provisions of the Statutory Declarations Act 1835

Declared at _____   Declarant to sign below

_____

_____

the _____ day of _____

One thousand nine hundred and _____

before me _____

A Commissioner for Oaths or Notary Public or Justice of
the Peace or Solicitor having the powers conferred on a
Commissioner for Oaths.

Presentor's name address and
reference (if any):

For official Use
New Companies Section   Post room

Appendix II

FRANCE: SPECIMEN DOCUMENTS

ARTICLES OF INCORPORATION

THE UNDERSIGNED

Represented by

THE FOLLOWING HAS BEEN AGREED:

The undersigned is to create a company with the following legal form.

ARTICLE 1 – FORM

The company is a limited company (SARL) and is subject to current law and to these articles of incorporation.

ARTICLE 2 – PURPOSE

The purpose of the company in France and abroad is:

ARTICLE 3 – NAME – INITIALS

The name of the company is:

All deed and documents issued by the company must include the words 'Société à Responsabilité Limitée' (limited liability company) or the initials S.A.R.L. immediately after the name of the company, as well as including details of the share capital.

ARTICLE 4 – TERM

The company will exist for a period of 99 years from the date of its registration with the Commercial Registry, unless wound up or extended.

ARTICLE 5 – REGISTERED OFFICE

The registered office of the company is:

The registered office may be transferred to any other address within the same town or neighbouring areas by simple decision of the management, the management then being authorised to amend these articles of incorporation accordingly. The registered office may be transferred to any other place by decision of an extraordinary general meeting of the shareholders.

ARTICLE 6 – INVESTMENT

The undersigned invested in the company, at the moment of its creation, all

[151]

of the share capital, i.e. a cash sum of FF 50,000.00, which sum has been deposited in an account in the name of the company to be created, in accordance with the law, with the following bank:

ARTICLE 7 – DISTRIBUTION OF SHARE CAPITAL

The share capital is fixed at FF 50,000.00 divided into 500 shares with a value of 100 francs each, fully paid up and allocated to the sole shareholder.

ARTICLE 8 – INCREASE OF CAPITAL

The share capital may be increased by any means authorised by the law and as a result of a collective extraordinary decision of the shareholders.

Where the increase in capital is made by means of an increase in the par value of existing shares, to be fully paid up, the shareholders' decision must be unanimous.

Any person becoming a shareholder by means of an increase in capital and who will be subject to approval as recipient of shares under Article 12 must be approved under the conditions provided by this article.

If the increase in capital is realised either in whole or in part by contributions in kind, the shareholders' decision voting the increase in capital and the corresponding amendment of the articles of incorporation must include an evaluation of the value of each contribution in kind by means of a report annexed to the said decision and prepared under the responsibility of an appraiser nominated in accordance with conditions set down by law.

ARTICLE 9 – REDUCTION OF CAPITAL

The capital may also be reduced by means of collective decision of the shareholders meeting within the conditions set down for amendment of the articles of incorporation, for whatever reason and in whatever manner, but any such reduction must not, under any circumstances, affect equality among the shareholders.

A reduction in share capital bringing the amount below the legal minimum may only be decided with the condition that an increase of capital will take place restoring the capital to the legal minimum, unless, at the same time, the company changes its legal form to a form not requiring a share capital higher than the reduced share capital. In the absence of such action, any interested party has the right to demand the liquidation of the company, two months after having served notice on the management requesting the regularisation of the situation.

The request for liquidation will not be granted if, on the day of the hearing, the situation has been regularised.

ARTICLE 10 – PAYING UP OF SHARES

Shares must be fully paid up before being allocated in return for cash or in-kind contributions.

ARTICLE 11 – REPRESENTATION OF SHARES

Shares can never be represented by negotiable, registered of bearer shares.

The rights of each shareholder derive entirely from these articles of incorporation, subsequent deeds amending the amount of share capital and any transfer of shares.

[152]

ARTICLE 12 – TRANSFER AND ASSIGNMENT OF SHARES

1.   The transfer of shares is effected either by a notarised deed or by private agreement. In order to be binding upon the company, notification of any such transfer should be made by bailiff, accepted by the company by means of a notarised deed or be deposited at the registered office of the company in accordance with the conditions set down by law. In order to be binding upon third parties, notification of any such transfer should also be deposited with the Court Clerk at the Commercial Registry.

2.   Shares can be freely transferred amongst shareholders, ancestors and heirs.

All other transfers of shares, as with all assignments of shares following death of the shareholder, liquidation of joint estate, or for reasons of merger, scission or investment, should have the prior authorisation of the majority of shareholders representing at least three quarters of the share capital.

The draft transfer, or notification of the death of a shareholder together with personal details of any beneficiaries, should be addressed to the company and to each of the shareholders by registered mail, return receipt requested, or served by the bailiff.

Within eight days of reception of such notification, the management invites all shareholders to decide on one of the forms provided for in Article 19.

If the company refuses to accept the transfer, the shareholders are obliged, within three months of the date of such refusal (to be made by registered letter, return receipt requested), to acquire or have acquired the shares at a price to be agreed between the parties or, in the absence of agreement, in accordance with the conditions set out in Article 1843–4 of the Civil Code.

The company can also, with the agreement of the shareholder transferring the shares and within the same time limits, decide to reduce the share capital by the amount of the par value of the shares in question and buy these shares at a price to be determined in accordance with the conditions set out above.

If, at the expiration of the said time limit, the company has not arranged for the purchase of the shares, the shareholder can conclude the proposed transfer.

However, any shareholder who has held shares for less than two years cannot take advantage of the provisions set out above. If, as a result of a transfer of shares, all shares constituting the share capital of the company are held by a single shareholder, the company will immediately become subject to the legal provisions applicable to single shareholder companies ('entreprises unipersonnelles a responsabilite limitee'), unless the transfer deed, or the resolution voted by the shareholders meeting approving the transfer, provide otherwise.

3.   Where the company has only one shareholder, the provisions of article 36–1 and 2 of the law of 24 July 1966 are applicable, i.e.:

–   if the single shareholder is a physical person, then this person cannot be the single shareholder of another SARL,

– if the single shareholder is another SARL, then this company must have more than one shareholder.

4. The transfer of shares, as defined by this article, includes all acts whose purpose or effect is the transfer of the ownership of shares with or without payment, by mutual agreement or otherwise, by public or private tender, voluntary or forced, by way of sale, investment or merger, donation, sharing and generally by any other means.

ARTICLE 13 – INDIVISIBILITY OF SHARES – SHAREHOLDERS RIGHTS

Shares are indivisible vis-a-vis the company. To exercise their rights, co-shareholders must represent themselves to the company by a common representative chosen either among them or from outside. In the absence of agreement, such representative will be nominated by the president of the commercial court, at the request of the most conscientious co-shareholder.

When calculating the majority amongst the shareholders, co-shareholders count for one shareholder where their rights come from a common origin.

ARTICLE 14 – RIGHTS AND OBLIGATIONS ATTACHED TO SHARES

Each share gives the shareholder the right to participate in all votes and discussions.

Each share gives its holder the right to a share in the profits and assets of the company in proportion to the total number of shares.

Within the limits of any responsibility resulting from the value placed on contributions in kind, a shareholder is only responsible for any debts up to the limit of the par value of shares held.

Ownership of a share implies acceptance of these articles of incorporation and of all collective decisions of the shareholders.

The rights and obligations attached to a share are unchanged by any transfer of ownership.

Heirs or creditors of a shareholder cannot, under any circumstances, either place the goods and documents of the company under seal or interfere in any manner with the administration of the company. To exercise their rights, they must refer to the company accounts and to the collective decisions of the shareholders.

Any increase in capital by the free allocation of shares may be made notwithstanding the existence of fractions of shares. Shareholders having an insufficient number of issuing rights to obtain the delivery of a new share must themselves acquire or transfer the necessary rights.

ARTICLE 15 – MANAGEMENT

The company is managed and administered by one or more managers, physical persons, shareholders or not, with or without limitations on their term of office, and chosen by the shareholders.

The first managers of the company are nominated by separate deed annexed to these articles of incorporation.

The managers can be re-elected.

The length of the mandate of the managers and any remuneration is contained in the deed nominating them.

The authority of the managers can also be limited by the deed nominating them.

Each manager has the right to sign on behalf of the company, within the limits of the preceding paragraph and the social purpose of the company.

The managers have the widest powers concerning relations with third parties to act on behalf of the company, only limited by those powers expressly reserved by law for the shareholders. Any manager, shareholder or not, can be removed by decision of the shareholders representing a majority of the share capital.

Each manager is responsible, under common law, to the company for any infringement of the law or of these articles for any management errors.

Any manager may renounce his functions by notifying the shareholders two months in advance by registered letter, unless a collective decision of the shareholders provides otherwise. In the event of the termination of management functions by one of the managers for whatever reason, the management of the company is assured by the remaining manager(s). The shareholders shall name one or more managers, at the request of a manager or one of the shareholders and in accordance with the conditions set out in article 18 below.

ARTICLE 16 – STATUTORY AUDITORS

The company is obliged to name a statutory auditor and deputy statutory auditor when, at the end of the financial year, two of the three following thresholds are exceeded:

- total balance sheet   10 million francs
- turnover before tax   20 million francs
- average number of   50
  employees

Further, one or more shareholders representing the minimum amount of share capital required by the law have the legal right to request the nomination of one or more statutory auditors.

The mandate of the statutory auditors runs for a period of six years, the mandate of the deputy statutory auditor being of the same duration of that of the statutory auditor.

The statutory auditors must fulfill the conditions and not be subject to any of the incapacities as defined by the law of 1 March 1985. They exercise their mandates and are remunerated in accordance with the law.

The company is not obliged to renominate statutory auditors, in the two years preceding the expiration of the mandate of the statutory auditors, if the company does not exceed the figures mentioned above for two of the three criteria.

The statutory auditors can be removed or challenged within the conditions set down by law.

ARTICLE 17 – COLLECTIVE DECISIONS

1. Where the company has several shareholders, the will of the shareholders is expressed by means of collective decisions which are binding on all shareholders, whether absent, dissident or incapacitated.

[155]

Such decisions can be made, at the discretion of the management, either by means of a general meeting or by written consultation. However, a general meeting is obligatory for approval of the accounts of each fiscal year.

All shareholders have the right to participate in all decisions, of whatever kind and regardless of the number of shares held, the number of votes equalling the number of shares held.

Each shareholder can be represented by another shareholder or by any other person in possession of a power of attorney.

A shareholder can be represented by a spouse unless the two together are the only shareholders. Unless there are only two shareholders, one shareholder can be represented by another. In all cases a shareholder can be represented by a third party in possession of a power of attorney.

The minutes of meetings are to be held either in a register (pages numbered and signed) or on loose leaves (also numbered and signed), as provided by law. Copies or extracts of these minutes can be declared certified copies by a manager.

Annual meeting

All general meetings are called by the management or, in default, by the statutory auditor, if any, or, in default of the above, by a representative appointed by the court at the request of any shareholder.

In a period of liquidation, the annual meetings are called by the liquidator.

The annual meetings are held at the registered office of the company or at any other place, in France or abroad, indicated in the notice of meeting. The notice of meeting is addressed by registered letter to the last known address of each shareholder at least fifteen days before the date of the meeting. This notice of meeting should contain the agenda for the meeting prepared by the person responsible for calling the meeting.

The meeting is chaired by one of the managers or, if neither manager is a shareholder, by the shareholder, present and accepting, representing the largest number of shares.

Only those items appearing on the agenda can be discussed.

Items discussed at the meeting are recorded in the form of minutes which should include any comments required by law and which should be prepared and signed by the manager(s) or, if necessary, by the president of the meeting.

In the absence of an attendance sheet, all shareholders must sign the minutes.

Written consultation

In the event of a written consultation, the management should send to each shareholder at the last known address any by registered letter, the text of proposed resolutions as well as any other documents necessary for the information of the shareholders.

The shareholders have a delay of fifteen days from receipt of the text of resolutions in which to cast their vote in writing. The vote, for each resolution, is either 'Yes' or 'No'.

Replies should be sent by registered letter. Any shareholder not replying within the time limit will be considered as abstaining.

2. When the company has only one shareholder, the single shareholder holds all the powers normally delegated to the annual shareholders meeting. In such a case, the provisions relating to communication obligations, the means of calling the meeting and quorum do not apply. A single shareholder cannot delegate powers.

ARTICLE 18 – ORDINARY COLLECTIVE DECISIONS

Ordinary collective decisions of the shareholders apply in all matters which do not fall within the exclusive competence of the management or of extraordinary collective decisions.

Such decisions are only valid if taken by shareholders representing more than half of the number of shares.

If this majority is not reached on the first consultation, the shareholders are consulted a second time and any decisions are valid if made by a majority of votes cast, no matter what proportion of the total number of shares are represented, but with the condition that only those matters presented in the first consultation appear in the second.

However, any decisions nominating or removing a manager must always be taken by shareholders representing more than half of the total number of shares.

ARTICLE 19 – EXTRAORDINARY COLLECTIVE DECISIONS

1. Extraordinary decisions are classified as those decisions taken by shareholders concerning approval of the transfer or assignment of shares or amendment of the articles of incorporation, within the limits of those exceptions set down by law.

2. Such extraordinary decisions are not validly taken unless made under the following conditions:

- by unanimous vote of shareholders if involving a change in the nationality of the company, increasing the undertakings of a shareholder or changing the company into either a general partnership, a limited partnership or a company limited by shares, or into a private company,
- by a majority of shareholders representing at least three quarters of the number of shares if the vote concerns the transfer or assignment of shares,
- by shareholders representing at least three quarters of the number of shares for all other extraordinary decisions.

ARTICLE 20 – SHAREHOLDERS RIGHT TO INFORMATION

1. Continuous

Each shareholder has the right at any time to inspect, at the registered office of the company, the following documents in respect of the preceding three fiscal years:

- annual accounts (balance sheet, results and annexes)
- inventories
- reports submitted to annual general meetings
- minutes of meetings.

The right to inspect these documents includes the right to take copies, with the exception of the inventories.

All shareholders have the right, at any time and on the day of the request, to obtain at the registered office of the company a certified copy of the current articles of incorporation.

2. Before annual meetings and consultations

At the time of all consultations of shareholders, either written or by way of annual meeting, each shareholder has the right to have knowledge of any documents or information necessary in order to make an informed vote and judge the management of the company.

The nature of these documents and the conditions under which they should be sent or made available to shareholders before the annual meeting are set out in article 23 below.

3. Emergency procedure

All shareholders have the right, twice a year, to pose written questions to the manager concerning any matter likely to compromise the future of the company. The reply should be communicated to the statutory auditor, if any.

4. Management experts

One or more shareholders representing at least the proportion of capital provided for by law can either individually or collectively ask the court to nominate one or more management experts whose mission will be to prepare a report on one or more aspects of the management of the company.

ARTICLE 21 – AGREEMENTS BETWEEN THE COMPANY AND THE SHAREHOLDERS OR MANAGERS

Within the limits of any legal constraints, agreements between the company and one of the shareholders or managers are subject to the formalities of control of the annual shareholders meeting, as provided for by law.

These formalities cover agreements concluded with any company where any shareholder, manager, director, managing director, member of the directorate or supervisory council is also manager or shareholder of that company.

In addition, shareholders can, with the agreement of the management and in accordance with conditions fixed by the latter, leave or deposit funds into a current account of the company which should not, under any circumstances, be in debit. No shareholder has the right to request the withdrawal of such sums without having warned the management at least one month in advance.

Agreements falling within the sphere of the purpose of the company as well as agreements concerning current operations and concluded under normal conditions are exempted from the formalities of control and presentation to the shareholders meeting mentioned above.

ARTICLE 22 – FISCAL YEAR

Each fiscal year will last for a period of twelve months beginning on the and ending on the of each year.

Exceptionally, the first fiscal year will begin with the registration of the company with the commercial registry and will end on

ARTICLE 23 – ACCOUNT DOCUMENTS
1.   Annual accounts

At the end of each fiscal year, the management prepares an inventory of the assets and liabilities of the company, a balance sheet summarising the inventory, the profit and loss account summarising the benefits and charges for the year and the annexe completing and commenting on the information provided in the balance sheet and the profit and loss account.

Even in the absence or insufficiency of profits, the management then allows for any depreciation and reserves provided for or authorised by the law.

The total of any amounts guaranteed, endorsed or secured by the company are listed at the end of the balance sheet.

The management prepares a management report concerning the previous fiscal year.

The annual accounts, management report, text of proposed resolutions and, where appropriate, the statutory auditor's report, consolidated accounts and the Group management report, should be addressed to the shareholders at least fifteen days before the date of the shareholders' meeting called to approve the accounts.

From this date, each shareholder has the right to present written questions to which the management must reply during the shareholders' meeting.

During the fifteen days preceding the date of the shareholders' meeting, the inventory is made available for inspection by the shareholders at the registered office. Copies of the inventory may not be made.

The above mentioned obligations to inform shareholders are not applicable where all shareholders are managers.

2.   Forward planning

When, at the end of the fiscal year, the company fulfils one of the following criteria:
- number of employees three hundred or more (employees concerned are those with an unlimited employment contract either directly with the company or with one of its subsidiaries, either direct or indirect), annual turnover before tax of 120 million francs or more, the manager or managers are required to prepare the following documents:

Each semester
- within four months of the end of each semester, the status of realisable and available assets, excluding stocks, and any due liabilities as well as the report of the manager or managers completing and commenting on the information contained in these documents.

Annually
- financial plan and annual accounts within four months of the end of the fiscal year,
- forward financial plan and profit and loss account, to be prepared at the latest at the end of the fourth month following the beginning of the new fiscal year (the profit and loss account is revised during the four months

[159]

following the beginning of the second semester of the fiscal year),
- report from the manager or managers completing and commenting on the information contained in the above mentioned documents.

The report of the manager or managers prepared each semester and annually should describe the accounting prnciples and methods used and hypotheses retained, as well as justifying their relevance and coherence.

All of the above mentioned documents should be transmitted to the statutory auditor and the 'comite d'enterprise', if any, within eight days of their completion.

ARTICLE 24 – ALLOCATION AND DISTRIBUTION OF PROFITS

The profit and loss account summarising the income and charges for the year, after deductions for depreciation and reserves, shows the profit for the fiscal year.

At least five percent of this profit, reduced where applicable by any previous losses, is deducted and added to the legal reserve. Such deduction is not obligatory once the reserves are equal to one tenth of the share capital. Deductions recommence when, for whatever reason, the reserve falls below one tenth of the share capital.

Distributable profits comprise the profits for the fiscal year, decreased by any previous losses and sums to be added to the reserve, in accordance with the law and these articles of incorporation, and increased by any profits carried forward.

Profits are allocated amongst the shareholders in proportion to the number of shares held. The annual shareholders' meeting can decide to distribute sums withdrawn from the reserves; the meeting must then expressly indicate from which part of the reserves such sums are to be withdrawn. However, dividends are by priority paid from the profits of the fiscal year in question. With the exception of reduction in capital, no distribution can be made to shareholders if the capital is or will be, as a result of such reduction, inferior to the amount of capital, increased by the reserves that the law or these articles of incorporation do now allow to be distributed. The reevaluation difference cannot be distributed. It can be either wholly or partially incorporated into the capital.

However, after deduction of sums to be added to the reserve, and in accordance with the law, the shareholders can, upon the recommendation of the management, decide to carry forward all or part of the profits they are entitled to or credit all or part of this amount to any general or special reserve they decide to create and decide the use of, if necessary.

Losses, if any, are either set off against any profits carried forward from previous years or carried forward.

ARTICLE 25 – PAYMENT OF DIVIDENDS

Payment of dividends must be effected within a maximum time limit of nine months after the end of the fiscal year, unless this time limit is extended by the courts.

Shareholders may not be required to repay dividends properly distributed.

Dividends remaining unclaimed after a period of five years are acquired by prescription by the company.

ARTICLE 26 – NET ASSETS LESS THAN SHARE CAPITAL

If, as a result of losses observed in the accounting documents, the net assets of the company are inferior to half of the share capital, the management must, in the four months following approval of the accounts showing this loss, consult the shareholders in order to decide whether the company should be dissolved.

If the dissolution is not decided, the capital, within the time limits set down by the law, must be reduced by an amount at least equal to the losses which could not be set off against the reserves, if, within the same time limit, it has not been possible to increase the net assets to at least half of the share capital.

ARTICLE 27 – PROROGATION OF THE COMPANY

At least one year before the expiry date of the company, the management must request a collective decision of the shareholders in order to decide, within the conditions regulating the making of extraordinary collective decisions, whether the life of the company will be extended or not. The shareholders' decision will, in all events, be made public.

In the absence of the necessary management act, any shareholders, irrespective of the number of shares held, can request the nomination, by the President of the commercial court, of a representative charged with consulting the shareholders and obtaining their response.

ARTICLE 28 – DISSOLUTION – LIQUIDATION

The company is dissolved at the end of its term (unless extended), by the total loss of its purpose, or by judicial decision for just cause.

The anticipated dissolution of the company can also result from an extraordinary collective decision of the shareholders. In the event of dissolution, for whatever reason, the company enters into liquidation.

ARTICLE 29 – DISPUTES

In the absence of any contrary agreement between the shareholders, all disputes concerning the interpretation of performance of these articles of incorporation or relating to the company's affairs, either between shareholders or between shareholders and the company, during the life of the company or during its liquidation, will be referred to the appropriate competent court.

ARTICLE 30 – TAKEOVER OF OBLIGATIONS UNDERTAKEN BEFORE REGISTRATION OF THE COMPANY

Before signature of these articles of incorporation, the acts listed in the attached annexe, together with an indication of their consequences for the company, were undertaken on behalf of the company in formation.

This list was deposited at the future registered office of the company for the information of future members of the company, the undersigned acknowledging.

This list will remain annexed to the articles of incorporation.

The registration of the company will entail the taking of automatic responsibility for the said obligations.

ARTICLE 31 – PUBLICITY – POWERS OF ATTORNEY

All powers are granted to   to effect all publication formalities relating to the formation of the company, and in particular:

- to sign the declaration provided for by article 6 of the commercial law
- to commence all formalities for the purposes of registering the company with the commercial registry.

ARTICLE 32 – TEMPORARY PROVISIONS

The two preceding articles, as well as this article, are only to be included in this original articles of incorporation. They will not be included in succeeding versions.

Signed on
(five copies)
The   day of   19..

Appendix III

DENMARK:
SPECIMEN DOCUMENTS

The undersigned

has under today's date founded a private limited company on the basis of the following articles of association:

ARTICLES OF ASSOCIATION
for

* * * * * * * * * * *

N.N. ApS

COMPANY NAME, REGISTERED OFFICE AND OBJECTS
ARTICLE 1.
   The company name shall be ***********
   The company shall have its registered office at Copenhagen Municipality.
ARTICLE 2.
   The objects of the company shall be to be engaged in trading and production.
ARTICLE 3.
   The share capital of the company shall be Kr 80,000.
ARTICLE 4.
   The company's general meeting will be held with a fortnight's notice to the shareholder.
   The agenda for the annual general meeting shall include:
1. Appointment of a chairman.
2. Presentation of annual accounts with auditing report for adoption and the annual report.
3. Proposal for distribution of profit or covering losses according to the adopted accounts.
4. Whether a director is to be elected.
5. Whether an accountant is to be elected.
6. Other business.

[163]

ARTICLE 5.

The company shall have no board of directors.

ARTICLE 6.

The company's accounts shall be audited by a chartered accountant elected by the general meeting. The auditor is appointed for a two year's period.

ARTICLE 7.

The financial year of the company shall be the calendar year.

ARTICLE 8.

The annual accounts shall be prepared in accordance with the Act on Preparation of Annual Accounts in force at any time

The shares are subscribed for and paid in full by the promoter.

The company will pay the cost in connection with the formation and is expected to amount to Kr 4,820 excluding VAT. The registration fee is Kr 2,020, capital investment tax Kr 800, fee to lawyers and printing etc. Kr 2,000.

Copenhagen,   1991

(The promoter's signature)

Appendix IV

IRELAND: SPECIMEN DOCUMENTS

COMPANIES ACTS, 1963 to 1986

COMPANY LIMITED BY SHARES

MEMORANDUM OF ASSOCIATION

- of -

1. The name of the Company is

2. The Objects for which the Company is established are:
    1. To carry on the business of manufacturers, distributors, importers and exporters (both wholesale and retail) of all classes and kinds of goods and merchandise, and to act as general agents in the buying, sale or transfer of goods and merchandise, and to carry on all or any of the businesses of importers, exporters, warehousemen, insurance brokers, carriers, forwarding agents, preservers and packers of provisions of all kinds; to carry on business as hotel keepers, lodging house and restaurant keepers, licensed vintners, transport agents, insurance agents; to act as property and business owners, builders and building contractors, land and estate developers, managers, consultants, developers of all classes of properties and estates, private, residential, commercial and equitable, of businesses of all kinds including retail, wholesale, import and export, hire purchase, commission agents, and transport of all kinds; to carry on business as electricians, painters, decorators, repairers, jobbers, carpenters, joiners, plumbers, merchants and manufacturers of and dealers in heating and electrical apparatus of all kinds and in articles, commodities and things of every description which may be required for the purpose of any

[165]

business which the Company is authorised to carry on or which are commonly dealt in by persons engaged in such business.

2. To carry on any other business (whether manufacturing or otherwise) of any description which may be capable of being advantageously carried on in connection with or ancillary to the objects of the Company or any of them.

3. To purchase, take on lease or in exchange, hire or otherwise acquire and hold for any estate or interest any lands, buildings, easements, rights, privileges, concessions, patents, patent rights, licenses, secret processes, machinery, plant, stock-in-trade, and any real or personal property of any kind necessary or convenient for the purposes of or in connection with the Company's business or any branch or department thereof.

4. To apply for, purchase or otherwise acquire any patents licenses or concessions which may be capable of being dealt with by the Company, or be deemed to benefit the Company and to grant rights thereout.

5. To erect, construct, lay down, enlarge, alter and maintain any shops, stores, factories, buildings, works, plant and machinery necessary or convenient for the Company's business, and to contribute to or subsidise the erection, construction and maintenance of any of the above.

6. To invest and deal with the monies of the Company not immediately required in such shares or upon such securities and in such manner as may from time to time be determined.

7. To enter into partnerships or into any arrangements for sharing profits, union of interests, co-operation, reciprocal concessions or otherwise, with any person or Company, carrying on business within the objects of this Company.

8. To sell or otherwise dispose of the whole or any part of the business or property of the Company.

9. To purchase or otherwise acquire all or any part of the business or assets of any person, firm or Company carrying on or formed to carry on any business which this Company is authorised to carry on or possessed of property suitable to the purposes of this Company and to pay cash or to issue any shares, stocks, debentures or debenture stock of this Company as the consideration for such purchase or acquisition and to undertake any liabilities or obligations relating to the property or business so purchased or acquired.

10. To guarantee, support or secure, whether by personal covenant or by mortgaging or charging all or any part of the undertaking, property and assets (present and future) and uncalled capital of the Company or by both such methods, and performance of the obligations of and the repayment or payment of the principal amounts of and premiums, interest and dividends on any securities of any person, firm or Company, including (without prejudice to the generality of the foregoing)

any Company which is for the time being the Company's Holding Company as defined by Section 155 of the Companies Act, 1963, or any subsidiary as defined by the said Section of the Company's Holding Company or otherwise associated with the Company in business.

11. To borrow and raise money in such manner as the Company shall think fit and in particular by the issue of debentures or debenture stock, mortgages, charges, perpetual or otherwise, charged upon all or any of the Company's property (both present and future) and undertaking, including its uncalled capital.

12. To draw, make, accept, endorse, discount, execute and issue negotiable or transferable instruments of all kinds.

13. To remunerate any person or company for services rendered or to be rendered in placing or assisting to place any of the shares in the Company's capital or any debentures, debenture stock, or other securities of the Company or in or about the formation of the Company or the conduct of its business.

14. To grant pensions, allowances, gratuities and bonuses to officers, or ex-officers, employees or ex-employees of the Company or its predecessors in business or the dependents of such persons and to establish and maintain or concur in maintaining trusts, funds or schemes (whether contributory or noncontributory) with a view to providing pensions or other funds for any such persons as aforesaid or their dependents.

15. To promote or aid in the promotion of any Company or Companies for the purpose of acquiring all or any of the property rights and liabilities of this Company or for any other purpose which may seem directly or indirectly calculated to advance the interests of this Company.

16. To distribute among the members in specie any property of the Company, or any proceeds of sale or disposal of any property of the Company, but so that no distribution amounting to a reduction of capital be made except with the sanction (if any) for the time being required by law.

17. To pay out of the funds of the Company all Costs and expenses of or incidental to the formation and registration of the Company and the issue of its capital and debentures including brokerage and commission.

18. To procure the Company to be registered or recognised in any country or place abroad.

19. To do all or any of the above things in any part of the world either alone or in conjunction with others and either as principals, agents, contractors, trustees, or otherwise, and either by or through agents, subcontractors, trustees or otherwise.

20. To lend, advance money, give credit to or become a surety or Guarantor for any person or Company and to give all descriptions of Guarantees and indemnities and either with or without the Company

receiving any consideration and/or any benefit to guarantee or otherwise secure whether by personal covenant or by mortgaging or changing all or any part of undertaking, property and assets present and future and the uncalled capital and goodwill of the Company or by both such methods, the performance of the obligations and the payment of the capital or principal of and dividends or interest on any stocks, shares, debentures, debenture stock, notes, bonds, loan agreements or other securities of any person, authority (whether supreme, local, municipal or otherwise) or Company including (without prejudice to the generality of the foregoing) any Company which is for the time being the Company's holding Company as defined by section 155 of the Companies Act 1963, or any Statutory modification or re-enactment thereof or another subsidiary (as defined by the said Section) of the Company's Holding Company or otherwise associated with the Company in business.

21. To do all such other things as are incidental or conducive to the above objects or any of them.
   IT IS HEREBY EXPRESSLY DECLARED that each Sub-Clause of this Clause shall be construed independently of the other Sub-Clauses hereof, and that none of the objects mentioned in any Sub-Clause shall be deemed to be merely subsidiary to the objects mentioned in any other Sub-Clause.

3. The liability of the members is Limited.

4. The Share Capital of the Company is £1*** divided into **** Shares of £** each, with power to increase the Share Capital. The Shares in the Original or any increased Share Capital may be divided into several classes and there may be attached thereto respectively any preferential deferred or other special rights, privileged, conditions or restrictions.

   WE, the several persons whose names, addresses and descriptions are subscribed, wish to be formed into a Company in pursuance of this Memorandum of Association and we agree to take the number of Shares in the Capital of the Company set opposite our respective names.

Names, addresses and descriptions of subscribers	Number of shares taken by each shareholder

Total Number of Shares taken

Dated the
Witness to the above Signatures:

(name and address
of witness)

COMPANIES ACTS, 1963 to 1986

COMPANY LIMITED BY SHARES

ARTICLES OF ASSOCIATION

- of -

PRELIMINARY
1. a) The Company is a Private Company within the meaning of Section 33 of the Companies Act 1963.
b) Regulations 8, 24, 51, 54, 84, 86 & 91 of Part 1 of Table A of the Companies Acts 1963 to 1983 shall not apply to the Company but the remaining Regulations of Part 1 of Table A as hereinafter modified together with the regulations contained in Part 11 of Table A (with the exception of Regulations 1 and 7) and the following Articles shall be the Regulations of the Company.
LIEN
2. The lien conferred by Regulation 11 of Part 1 of Table A shall apply to all shares of the Company whether fully paid or not and to all shares registered in the name of any person indebted or under liability to the Company whether he be the sole registered holder thereof or shall be one of several joint holders. Regulations 11 of Part 1 of Table A shall be varied accordingly.
GENERAL MEETINGS
3. The words 'one member' shall be substituted for the words 'two members' in Regulation 50 of Part 1 of Table A.
4. The word 'two' shall be substituted for the word 'three' in Regulation 59(b) of Part 1 of Table A.
DIRECTORS
5. Unless and until otherwise determined by the Company in General Meeting the number of Directors shall be not less than two nor more than seven, and Regulation 75 shall be modified accordingly.

[169]

6.   Provided that he shall declare his interest in any Contract or transaction a Director may vote as Director with regard to any contract or transaction in which he is interested or in respect of his appointment to any office or place of profit or upon any matter arising thereout and if he shall so vote his vote shall be counted. This article is in substitution for Regulation 7 of Part 11 of Table A.

7.   The Office of a Director shall be vacated:

  a) If by notice in writing to the Company he resigns the office of Director.

  b) If he becomes bankrupt or enters into any arrangement with his creditors.

  c) If he becomes of unsound mind.

  d) If he is prohibited from being a Director by any Order made under Section 184 of the Act.

  e) If he is removed from office by a Resolution duly passed under Section 182 of the Act.

BORROWING POWERS

8.   The Directors may exercise all the powers conferred upon them by Regulation 79 of Part 1 of Table A without any limit on the amount for the time being remaining undischarged of money so borrowed or secured and the proviso limiting such amount contained in that Regulation shall not apply.

NAMES AND ADDRESSES and DESCRIPTIONS of SUBSCRIBERS

Dated the

WITNESS to the above Signatures:

(name and address
of witness)

Companies Registration Office

Statement of first secretary and directors and situation of registered office Section 3 of Companies (Amendment) Act 1982	Companies Acts 1963 to 1986	Registration fee stamp to be affixed above
Declaration of compliance Section 5 of Companies (Amendment) Act 1983	Company number	
Companies capital duty statement Section 69 of Finance Act 1973		**A1**

Please complete using black block capitals or typewriting

Company name *in full*

_____

_____ Limited

Note one
Maximum number of characters per line is thirty. Please leave one space between words

Address of registered office *note one*

If the memorandum is delivered by an agent for the subscribers of the memorandum mark 'x' in this box ☐ and insert the agents name and address

Agent's name

Agent's address

Number of continuation sheets attached

Particulars of secretary

Names and particulars of the person/s who is/are to be secretary/joint secretaries

Note two
Insert full name (initials will not suffice) and residential address. Where there are joint secretaries, details and signature of consent should be annexed hereto

Name *note two*

Note three
Former names do not include the following

In the case of a person known by a title different from his/her surname, the name by which he was known prior to the adoption of the title;

A name that has been changed before the person attained the age of 18 years, or a name that has been changed or disused for 20 years or more.

The name of a married woman, prior to her marriage.

Former name *note three*

Address *note two*

I hereby consent to act as secretary of the aforementioned company

Signature   Date

Presenter's name   Address

Reference

[171]

Particulars of Directors

Names and particulars of the persons who are
to be the first directors of the company

Name *note two*   Business occupation

Former name/s *note three*

Home address

                           Nationality if not Irish

Note four
Company number and
name of other bodies
corporate in the State of
which the director of the
company is also a
director should be given,
except for the following

Bodies corporate of
which the company is a
wholly owned
subsidiary.

Bodies corporate which
are wholly owned
subsidiaries of the
company or of the
company's parent
company

Particulars of other directorships *note four*   Company number

*I hereby consent to act as director of the
aforementioned company*

Signature   Date

Name *note two*   Business occupation

Former name/s *note three*

Home address

                           Nationality if not Irish

Particulars of other directorships *note four*   Company number

*I hereby consent to act as director of the
aforementioned company*

Signature   Date

Name *note two*   Business occupation

Former name/s *note three*

Home address

                           Nationality if not Irish

Particulars of other directorships *note four*   Company number

*I hereby consent to act as director of the
aforementioned company*

Signature   Date

Name *note two*   Business occupation

Former name/s *note three*

Home address

                           Nationality if not Irish

Particulars of other directorships *note four*   Company number

*I hereby consent to act as director of the
aforementioned company*

Signature   Date

APPENDIX IV

Name *note two*   Business occupation
_____

Former name/s *note three*
_____
Home address
_____

                                                    Nationality if not Irish
_____
Particulars of other directorships *note four*   Company number
_____
_____
_____

I hereby consent to act as director of the
aforementioned company

Signature   Date
_____

Name *note two*   Business occupation
_____

Former name/s *note three*
_____
Home address
_____

                                                    Nationality if not Irish
_____
Particulars of other directorships *note four*   Company number
_____
_____
_____

I hereby consent to act as director of the
aforementioned company

Signature   Date
_____

Name *note two*   Business occupation
_____

Former name/s *note three*
_____
Home address
_____

                                                    Nationality if not Irish
_____
Particulars of other directorships *note four*   Company number
_____
_____
_____

I hereby consent to act as director of the
aforementioned company

Signature   Date
_____

Signed by or on behalf of the subscribers to
the memorandum

Signature   ☐ Subscriber ☐ Agent   Date
_____
Signature   ☐ Subscriber ☐ Agent   Date
_____
Signature   ☐ Subscriber ☐ Agent   Date
_____
Signature   ☐ Subscriber ☐ Agent   Date
_____
Signature   ☐ Subscriber ☐ Agent   Date
_____
Signature   ☐ Subscriber ☐ Agent   Date
_____
Signature   ☐ Subscriber ☐ Agent   Date
_____

Declaration of compliance

I name   of home address

do solemnly and sincerely declare that I am (note five)

of company

and that all the requirements of the Companies Acts, 1963 to
1983 in respect of the registration of the said company, and of
matters precedent and incidental thereto have been complied
with.   Declared before me by
And I make this solemn declaration conscientiously believing
the same to be true and by virtue of the Statutory Declarations
Act, 1938.   who is personally known to me or who is
                  identified to me by
Signature of Declarant

                              who is personally known to me at
Commissioner for Oaths

☐ Commissioner for Oaths
☐ Notary Public ☐ Peace Commissioner   this   day of   19

Companies capital duty statement

Effective centre of management if outside the state

Class note six	Nominal value of each share class	No of shares authorised	No of shares being allotted

Consideration for each share note seven   Total number

I the undersigned (name)

furnish these particulars as (description)

Signed   Address

                                    Date

[174]

Appendix V

LUXEMBOURG:
SPECIMEN DOCUMENTS

In the year one thousand nine hundred and ninety-
Before   notary, residing in

There appeared:

Such appearing parties have decided to form amongst themselves a company
in accordance with the following Articles of Incorporation.

ARTICLE 1.
   There is hereby formed a company (societe a resonsabilite limitee) under the
name of
   The registered office is established in Luxembourg. It may be transferred to
any other place within the Grand-Duchy of Luxembourg by a resolution of the
Board of Directors.
   The company is formed for an unlimited period to run from this date.
ARTICLE 2.
   The purpose of the company will be the provision of consultancy services for
and the promotion of trading in all manner of goods and services, the acquisition and management of companies, business undertakings and part of such
undertakings which are engaged in the production and marketing of those
products or substitution products.
   The company may carry out any transactions of a commercial, industrial,
financial, movable real kind which may be related directly or indirectly to its
object.
ARTICLE 3.
   The corporate capital is fixed at one hundred thousand Luxembourg Francs
(00,000 – F.lux), dividend into one hundred (00) shares having a par value of
one thousand Luxembourg francs (.000 – F.lux) each.

These shares have been allocated to the shareholders in proportion with their contribution i.e.:

These amounts have been fully paid up in cash by the shareholders and proof thereof has been given to the undersigned notary who expressly requested this.

The capital may be changed at any time under the conditions specified by article 199 of the law covering companies.

ARTICLE 4.

The company's shares are freely transferable between shareholders. They may only be disposed of to new shareholders at a general meeting of shareholders and with a majority vote representing three quarters of the share capital.

ARTICLE 5.

The death, suspension of civil rights, insolvency or bankruptcy of one of the shareholders will not bring the company to an end.

ARTICLE 6.

Each share shall confer on its holder an equal right, in proportion to the number of existing shares, in the Company profit and the Company assets.

ARTICLE 7.

Management. The Company shall be managed by a board of Directors composed at least of three members appointed by the General Meeting of Shareholders for a period of six years and removed from office 'ad nutum' by the General Meeting. Retiring directors may be reelected.

The Board of Directors will act as a collective body.

The Board will have full powers regarding the administration and management of the company and for the accomplishment of the object of the company. Remuneration of Directors shall be set by the General Meeting of Shareholders.

The company will be bound by the joint signatures of two Directors.

ARTICLE 8.

The Board of Directors may delegate the daily management of the Company's business to one of several Managing Directors to be elected from among its members.

The Board may further entrust one or several Directors, General Managers, Managers or special authorised Company Officers with the whole or part of its missions and will determine the responsibilities and remunerations which may be fixed or variable with or without sharing in the Company profits, the duration and any other relevant conditions.

ARTICLE 9.

The Board of Directors shall elect from among its members a Chairman and a Secretary with the latter eligible from outside the Board.

The Board of Directors shall meet upon the request of the Chairman, Meetings of the Board of Directors must be called at least 15 days in advance of the day set for such a meeting. The Board of Directors may be called to meet if at least two Directors so request and the meeting shall take place during the month of such request. The Board of Directors shall meet in such places as shall be set forth in the notice.

ARTICLE 10.

The meetings of the Board of Directors shall be presided over by the Chairman, or any other Director appointed to chairmanship by his colleagues.

The Board of Directors can deliberate validly only if at least a majority of the Directors is present or represented. The Directors may vote in writing, by telex or by fax.

The Directors may appoint in writing, by telex or by fax any other Director as his proxy to represent them at the meeting and vote in their name and, while each member may not represent more than one Director. Proxies shall be attached to the minutes of the Board of Directors. All resolutions shall be taken by an absolute majority of the members present or represented on the Board of Directors.

The proceedings of a Board of Directors shall be recorded by minutes written in a register which shall be kept at the registered office of the Company. The minutes shall be signed by all members present at the meeting.

Copies or extracts of such minutes shall be certified by the Chairman, or by two Directors.

ARTICLE 11.

Supervision. Supervision and scrutiny of the transactions of the Company shall be entrusted to one or several auditors which may be shareholders or not and which are appointed by the General Meeting of Shareholders which also determines their remuneration. Auditors, other than one of the shareholders or one of their personnel must have the qualification of chartered accountant.

The statutory auditor shall hold office for six years.

ARTICLE 12.

Each shareholder may take part in collective decisions irrespective of the number of shares which he owns. Each shareholder has voting rights commensurate with his shareholding. Each shareholder may appoint a proxy to represent him at meetings.

ARTICLE 13.

Collective decisions are only validly taken in so far as they are adopted by shareholders owning more than half of the share capital. However, resolutions to alter the articles and particularly to liquidate the company may only be carried by a majority of shareholders owning at least three quarters of the company's share capital.

ARTICLE 14.

The company's year commenced on the first of January and ends on the thirty-first of December. The first financial year commences this day and ends on the thirty-first of December nineteen hundred and

ARTICLE 15.

Each year on the thirty-first of December the books are closed and the directors prepare an inventory including an indication of the value of the company's assets and liabilities.

ARTICLE 16.

Each shareholder may inspect the above inventory and balance sheet at the company's registered office.

ARTICLE 17.

The receipts stated in the annual inventory, after deduction of general expense and amortisation, represents the net profit.

Five per cent of the net profit is set aside for the establishment of a statutory reserve, until this reserve amounts to ten per cent of the share capital. The balance may be used freely by the shareholders.

ARTICLE 18.

At the time of the winding up of the company the liquidation will be carried out by one of several liquidators, shareholders or not, appointed by the shareholders who will fix their powers and remuneration.

ARTICLE 19.

The shareholders will refer to legal provisions on all matters to which no specific provision is made in the articles. The undersigned notary states that the specific conditions of article 183 of company law act (Companies Act of 18.9.1933) are satisfied.

Estimate of costs

The parties estimate the value of formation expenses at approximately forty-five thousand francs (45,000).

Extraordinary general meetings

With the articles of incorporation thus drawn up, the above named persons have immediately proceeded to hold an extraordinary general meeting and have passed the following resolutions by unanimous vote:

1. The number of Directors shall be set at three.

    The following are elected Directors:

    a) Mr.

    b) Mr.

    c) Mr.

2. The statutory auditor elected is:

in Luxembourg.

The undersigned notary who knows English, states herewith that on request of the above appearing persons the binding incorporation deed is worded in French, followed by an English version; on request of the same appearing persons and in case of divergences between the English and the French text, the French version will be binding.

Appendix VI

EUROPEAN ECONOMIC INTEREST
GROUPINGS (EEIGs)

An EEIG is a new form of business organisation created by a European Community Council Regulation, and is a common legal concept throughout the member states. (Its actual name may vary from state to state.)

It must have a minimum of two members, who have their central administration or principal activities in different member states of the EC. If it has more than two members then some of its members may be from the same state. As long as they are EC based, then the members can be individuals, companies, firms or other legal bodies.

An EEIG can act very much the same as an incorporated company, but its members will have unlimited joint and several liability. It is formed by a contract (which must be registered) and must include: names, addresses, objects and duration (can be indefinite). After this, the contents of the contract can be flexible and designed as the members wish. The purpose of an EEIG creation as a legal concept is to contribute to effective cooperation between members, carrying on commercial activities within different member states.

Some uses of an EEIG
    joint purchasing
    distribution
    research and development
    manufacturing and assembly
    purchasing
    tendering for a major works project

Advantages
- Its structure is very flexible.
- It has the capacity to do things in its own name, as an incorporated company would do.
- It has flexibility, in that it is designed and regulated by a contract between its members, very much like a partnership.

[179]

- It is recognised in all member states of the EC.
- It does not require a fixed capital contribution.
- It offers similar advantages to a jointly owned subsidiary.
- Alterations to the contract are optional.
- It is easier to operate internationally.
- It adds stature to the business and creates a European image.

Disadvantages
- Unlimited joint and several liability for the debts.
- A creditor can proceed against one member for the full debt.
- Taxation considerations may effect the apparent flexibility of the EEIG.
- Restrictions on the activities can make the EEIG unsuitable for certain ventures.
- It cannot employ more than five hundred people.

Registration formalities
The following pages list the registration formalities for each of the member states of the European Community, except for Italy, Greece and Luxembourg (see note under appropriate country heading).

Belgium   **Commencement Date:** 22 August 1989

Name: Europees Economisch Samenwerkingsverband/Groupement.
Européen d'Interet Economique (EESV/GEIE).
Documents: Formation Agreement, executed by notarial deed or by private deed.
Forms: *Formule I*   (French).
Formulier I   (Flemish).

The formation agreement and form must be filed within fifteen days of execution of agreement. Registration fees are BF2,400 per page. Evidence of Registration: within five days after filing, registration details are published in the *Belgisch Staatsblad/Moniteur Belge*. The details must also be sent for publication in the Official Journal of the European Communities within one month of publication in the Belgian Official Gazette.
Information Address:
Rechtbank van Koophandel/Tribunal de Commerce, rue Paul Devauxstraat 5, B–1000 Brussel/Bruxelles
Tel: 32 2512 7448 or 32 2512 7512

Denmark

Commencement Date: 5 April 1989

Name: Europaeiske okonomiske firmagrupper (EOFG).
Documents: Formation Agreement.
Forms: *Anmeldelse til Erhvervs-eg Selskabsstyrelsen* register for *europaeiske okonomiske firmagrupper.*

The formation agreement and forms must be filed within four weeks of execution of Agreement. Evidence of Registration: Registration number and certificate are issued. Notice of registration is published in the *Statstidende* and the Official Journal of the European Communities (*EF-Tidende*). Registration fees are Kr 1700.
Information Address:
Registrar of Companies,
Erhvervs-eg Selskabsstyrelsen,
Kampmannsgade 1,
DK-Copenhagen, 1604 V
Denmark
Tel 33 124280   Fax: 33 324480

Republic of Ireland

Commencement Date: 1 August 1989

Name: European Economic Interest Grouping/Grpail Eorpach um Leas Eacnamaioch (EEIG/GELE).
Documents: Formation Agreement.
Forms: IG1, IG5.

The formation agreement and forms to be filed within 14 days of execution. Registration fee is IR£150. Evidence of Registration: The registrar issues a Certificate of Registration. The EEIG must publish as set out in the Irish *Oifigiuil* within 21 days. Publication in the Official Journal of the European Communities is carried out by the registrar.
Information Address:
Companies Registration Office,
Lower Castle Yard,
Dublin Casle,
Dublin 2, Ireland
Tel: 353 1614222

France

Commencement Date: 13 June 1989

Name: Groupement Européen d'Interet Economique (GEIE)

Documents: Two copies of the formation Agreement.
Two copies of any separate documents naming the Managers (unless included in the formation agreement).
Birth certificates of the manager(s) and financial controller(s).
The K-bis statements of Members which are French corporate bodies.
Certified copies of the bylaws of foreign corporate bodies.
Marriage contracts and other personal information of Members who are private individuals, both foreign or French. A complete list can be obtained from CFE.

Forms: C1.

Registration fee is approx. FF 1,190 plus a set of tax of 1%, on any capital or assets. Evidence of Registration: Initial publication in the local Gazette. Advertisement in the Official Bulletin of civil and commercial notices (BODACC) and in the Official Journal of the European Communities. A statement of compliance is issued by registrar on registration.

Information Address:
Le Centre des Formalités d'Entreprises, (CFE),
Chambre de Commerce de l'Ile-de-France,
1 Quai de Corse,
F-75004 Paris, France
Tel: 33 1 43 29 12 60

Great Britain and Northern Ireland

Commencement Date:
UK Regulations – 1 July 1989
NI Regulations – 17 July 1989

Name: European Economic Interest Grouping (EEIG).
Documents: Formation Agreement.
Forms: EEIG 1.

The formation agreement and form EEIG 1 to be delivered within 15 days of execution of agreement. Registration fee £50. Evidence of Registration: Registrar issues certificate of Registration. He then publishes an advertisement in the London, Edinburgh or Belfast Gazette and the Official Journal of the European Communities.

Information Addresses:
(for England & Wales)
Companies House,
Crown Way,
Maindy,
Cardiff, CF4 3UZ
Tel: 44 222 380529

(for Northern Ireland)
Companies House,
IDB House,
64 Chichester Street,
Belfast, BT1 4JX
Tel: 44 232 234488

(for Scotland)
Companies House,
102 George Street,
Edinburgh, EH2 3DJ
Tel: 44 31 225 5774

Greece

Greece is presently amendings its Commercial Code and there are no details available.

Italy and Luxembourg

No registration procedure has been implemented at the time of writing.

Netherlands   Commencement Date: 1 July 1989

Name: Europees Economisch Samenwerkingsverband (EESV).
Documents: Original or authenticated Formation Agreement.
Forms: Available on request.

No set time limits at present for filing. Registration fees are on a scale dependent on the capital. Evidence of Registration: Details of the EESV must be published in the Dutch Government Gazette – *De Nederlandse Staatscourant* and the Official Journal of the European Communities.
Information Address:
Handelsregister van de Kamer van,
Koophandel en Fabrieken te Amsterdam (Commercial Registry)
Koningin Wilhelminaplein 13,
NL-1062 HH Amsterdam
Tel: 31 20 172882   Fax: 31 20 172493

Portugal

Commencement Date: 8 June 1990

Name: Agrupamento Europeu de Interesse Economico (AEIE).
Documents: Formation Agreement.
Forms: Available on request.

The Formation Agreement must be filed within 90 days of execution.
Registration fees depend on whether it is Portuguese or not. Evidence of Registration: Commercial registrar publishes formation agreement in the Diario de Republica and registration at the Registo Nacional de Pessoas Colectivas. It is also published in the Official Journal of the European Communities.
Information Address:
Conservatoria do Registo Comercial,
Rua Nova do Almada 35,
1200 Lisboa, Portugal.
Tel: 351 3461556

Spain

Commencement Date: 1 January 1990

Name: Agrupacion Europea de Interes Economico (AEIE).
Documents: Formation Agreement duly notarised and translated into Spanish if required.
Forms: Application for Registration.
Deposit for publication.
Application for legislation of statutory books.

Registration fees depend on capital. Evidence of Registration: Published in the *Boletin Oficial del Registro Mercantil* and the Official Journal of the European Communities.
Information Address:
Registro Mercantil,
Principe de Vergara 72, Bajos
E-28006 Madrid, Spain
Tel: 34 1 411 39 05   Fax: 34 1 411 09 05

Germany

Commencement Date: 1 July 1989

Name: Europaische wirtschaftliche interessenvereinigung (EWIV).
Documents: Formation Agreement.
Forms: Available on request.

No set time limits for filing. Registration fees are approx DM600–800. Evidence

[184]

of Registration: Publication in the federal official gazette or *Bundesanzeiger*, and in the Official Journal of the European Communities.
Information Address:
Handelsregister,
Amtsgericht Frankfurt am Main,
Gerichtstrasse 2 (Gebaude B),
D-6000 Frankfurt 1
Tel: 49 69 136701

Appendix VII

USEFUL ADDRESSES

There are over 200 European Information Centres in Europe, however I have only included three for each country based in the main towns.

Germany

European information centres
R.K.W. (Rationalisierungs-Kuratorium der Deutschen Wirschaft), European Information Centre, Heilwigstrasse 33, D-2000 Hamburg 20. Tel: 49 40 4602087.

D.I.H.T. (Deutscher Industrie und Handelstag), European Information Centre, Adenauerallee 148, Postfach 1446, D-5300 Bonn 1. Tel: 49 228 1040.

Berliner Absatz-Organisation GmbH, European Information Centre, Hardenberstrasse 16–18, 1000 Berlin 12. Tel: 49 30 31 80 1.

Other useful addresses
German Chamber of Industry and Commerce, 12/13 Suffolk Street, St James's, London SW1Y 5HG. Tel: 071 930 7251.

British Chamber of Commerce in Germany, Secretariat Heumarkt 14, D-5000 Cologne 1.

The German Embassy, 23 Belgrave Square, London SW1X 8PZ.

British Overseas Trade Board – German Desk, 1–19 Victoria Street, London SW1H 0ET. Tel: 071 215 4796.

Italy

European information centres
European Information Centre, Camera di Commercio Industria Artigianato e Agricoltura di Milano, Via Delle Orsole 4/B, I-20143 Milano. Tel: 39 2 85154456.

European Information Centre, Camera di Commercia Industria Artigianato e Agricoltura di Napoli, Corso Meridionale 58, I-80143 Napoli. Tel: 39 81 269897.

Confederazione Generale Italiana del Commercio e del Turismo, European Information Centre, Piassa G.G. Belli 2, 00153, Roma. Tel: 39 6 5898973/ 5897613.

Other useful addresses
Ministero Industrie E Commercio, D G Produzione Industriale, Via Vittorio Veneto 33, 00100 Roma.

The Embassy of Italy, 14 Three, Kingsyard, London W1.

Commercial Department, British Consulate-General, Via San Paolo 7, I-20121, Milan. Tel: 392 8693442.

British Chamber of Commerce in Italy, Via Tarchetti 1, I-20121 Milan.

Ministeri de Tesoro, Via XX Settembre 97, I-00187, Rome.

Department of Trade and Industry – Italian Desk, 1–19 Victoria Street, London SW1H 0ET. Tel: 071 215 5103.

United Kingdom

European Information centres
Centre of European Business Information, Small Firms Service, 11 Belgrave Road, London SW1V 1RB. Tel: 071 828 6201.

Local Entreprise Development Unit, European Information Centre, Ledu House, Upper Galwally, Belfast, BT8 4TB. Tel: 0232 491031.

European Information Centre, Scottish Development Agency, 120 Bothwell Street, Glasgow, G2 6NR. Tel: 041 2210999.

European Information Centre, Birmingham Chamber of Industry and Commerce, 75 Harborne Road, PO Box 360, Birmingham B15 3DH. Tel: 021 454 6171.

Company formation office
Company Registration Office, Companies House, Crown Way, Maindy, Cardiff CF4 3UZ.

Other useful addresses
British Overseas Trade Board, 1 Victoria Street, London, SW1H 0ET.

EC Affairs, 41 Lothbury, London, EC2P 2BP. Tel: 071 726 1174.

The Department of Trade and Industry, Hints to Exporters Unit, Lime Grove, Eastcote, Ruislip, Middlesex, HA4 8SG.

Department of Trade and Industry, Export Intelligence Service, Lime Grove, Ruislip, Middlesex, HA4 8SG.

Department of Trade and Industry, 1–19 Victoria Street, London, SW1H 0ET. Tel: 071 215 4357.

European Parliament, 2 Queen Anne's Gate, London, SW1H 9AA. Tel: 071 222 0411.

European Commission, 8 Storey's Gate, London, SW1P 3AT. Tel: 071 222 8122.

Chamber of Commerce (Invest in Britain Bureau), Victoria Street, London, SW1H 0ET. Tel: 071 215 2501.

France

European information centres
Comité D'Expansion Aquitaine, European Information Centre, Place de la Bourse 2, F-33076 Bordaeux Cedex. Tel: 33 56 526547/529894.

Chambre Regionale de Commerce et D'Industrie de Bourgogne, European Information Centre, Rue Chevreul 68, BP 209, 21006 Dijon. Tel: 33 80 63 52 63.

Centre Francais du Commerce Extérieur, European Information Centre, 10 Avenue d'Iena, F-75783 Paris 16. Tel: 33 1 40 73 30 00.

Other useful addresses
Clerk of the Commercial Court, Registre du Commerce, 1 Boulevard de Palais, 75001 Paris.

The Embassy of France, 21–24 Grosvenor Place, London, SW1X 7HU.

The British Embassy, 35 rue du Faubourg-Saint-Honoré, 75009 Paris.

Franco-British Chamber of Commerce and Industry, 8 rue Cimarosa, 75116 Paris. Tel: 45 05 13 08.

French Industrial Development Board, 21–24 Grosvenor Place, London, SW1X 7HU. Tel: 071 823 1895.

Registre du Commerce (Paris and Greater Paris areas), 1 boulevard du Palais, 75001 Paris. Tel: 43 29 12 60.

Ministry of Labour/Social Security, Direction Générale de la Securité Sociale, 1 place de Fontenoy, 75007 Paris. Tel: 45 67 54 00.

Service des Relations Extérieures, 97–101 rue de Grenelle, 75007, Paris. Tel: 45 55 93 00.

Direction de l'Expansion Industrielle, 68 rue de Bellechasse, 75007 Paris. Tel: 454 48 44 30.

Institut National de la Propriété Industrielle, 26 bis rue de Leningrad, 75008 Paris. Tel: 45 22 52 90.

Department of Trade and Industry – French Desk, 1–19 Victoria Street, London, SW1H 0ET. Tel: 071 215 4668.

French Industrial Development Board, 21–24 Grosvenor Place, London, SW1X 7HU. Tel: 071 222 8122.

Spain

European information centres
Centre D'Informacio I Desenvolupament Empresarial (CIDEM), European Information Centre, c/o Cidem, Av Diagonal 403 Ir, E-08008 Barcelona. Tel: 34 3 2172008.

Camera Oficial de Comercio Industria y Navegacion de Bilbao, European Information Centre, Alameda de Recalde 50, E-48008 Bilboa. Tel: 34 3 4444054.

Confederacion Espanola de Prganizaciones de Empresarios, European Information Centre, Diego de Leon 50, 28006 Madrid. Tel: 34 1 5639641.

Other useful addresses
Spanish Embassy, 22 Manchester Square, London, W1M 5AP.

Spanish Chamber of Commerce, 5 Cavendish Square, London, W1. Tel: 071 637 9061.

Department of Trade and Industry – Spanish Desk, 1–19 Victoria Street, London, SW1H 0ET. Tel: 071 215 5526.

The Netherlands

European information centres
EIC Zuid-Holland, The Hague Chamber of Commerce and Industry, Alexander Gogelweg 16, PO Box 29718, 2517 JH. The Hague. Tel: 31 70 79 52 80.

Vereniging Van Kamers Van Koophandel, European Information Centre, Watermolenlaan 1, 3440 Woerden. Tel: 31 34 80 26 911.

Aktieprogramma Regionale Economie (A.R.E.), European Information Centre, 271 Postbus, Kasteellaan 9 DA, 6600 Wijchen. Tel: 31 88 94 23 457.

Other useful addresses
Central Institute for Medium and Small Sized Businesses, Dalsteindreef 9, 1112 XC Diemen.

Coordinating Foundation for Maintaining Service-Supply Centres for Small Businesses, Dalsteindreef 9, 1112 XC Diemen.

Economic Institute for Medium and Small Sized Businesses, Neuhuyskade 94, 2509 LR, The Hague.

De Vereniging van Kamers van Kopphandel en Fabrieken in Nederland, Waterstraat 47, 3511 BW Utrecht.

Royal Netherlands Embassy, 38 Hyde Park Gate, London, SW7 5DP.

De Vereniging van Kamers van Koophandel en Fabrieken in Nederland, Waterstraat 47, 3511 BW Utrecht.

The Netherlands Foreign Investment Agency, Office for Europe, PO Box 20101, 2500 EC, The Hague. Tel: 31 70 797029.

Amsterdam Chamber of Commerce and Industry, Wilheiminaplein 12, 1062 HH Amsterdam.

Dutch Chamber of Commerce, Alexander Gogelweg 16, 2517 JH Den Haag. Tel: 31 70 795 795.

Vereniging van Kamers van Koophandel en Fabrieken in Nederland, Watermolenlaan 1, 3447 GT Woerden. Tel: 3480 26911.

Belgium

European information centres
European Information Centrum, Kamer van Koophandel en Nijverheid, Van Antwerpen, Markgravestraat 12, B-2000 Antwerpen. Tel: 32 3 2337568.

European Information Centre Brussels, Avenue Louise 500, B-1050 Bruxelles. Tel: 32 3 6485002.

Institut Provincial des Classes Moyennes, European Information Centre, BD D'Avroy 28-30, 4000 Leige. Tel: 32 41 23 38 40.

Other useful addresses
Commission des Normes Comtables, Avenue Louise 99, 1050 Bruxelles (control body of company accounts).

The Centrale des Bilans, Banque Nationale de Belgique, Boulevarde de Berlaimont 5, 1000 Bruxelles. Tel: 02 221 4545. (Hold records of all companies registered in Belgium through the local commercial court).

Société Ori-Database, Place de l'Université 16, 1348 Louvain-La-Neuve. (Private Company that holds information on all registered companies).

The Embassy of Belgium, 103 Eaton Square, London, SW1W 9AB.

Federation Royale des Notaries de Belgique, rue de la Montagne 30–32, 1000 Bruxelles.

British Chamber of Commerce of Belgium, Rue Joseph II, 30 Jozef II strat, 1040 Bruxelles. Tel: 32 2 219 0787.

Commission des Normes Comptables, Avenue Louise 99, 1050 Bruxelles. Tel: 02 535 2211.

Société ORI-DATABASE, Place de l'Université 16, 1348 Louvain-La-Neuve. Tel: 10 47 6711.

Ministry of Economic Affairs: Economic Expansion and Foreign Investment Service, Square de Meeus 23, 1040 Bruxelles. Tel: 2 511 19 30.

Greece

European information centres
Chambre de Commerce et D'Industrie D'Athenes, European Information Centre, 7 Academias, GR-10671 Athinai. Tel: 30 1 3627337.

Hellenic Organization of Small and Medium Size Industries and Handicrafts (EOMMEX), European Information Centre, Xenias Street 16, GR-11528 Athina. Tel: 30 1 7794229.

Chambre of Commerce of Iraklion, European Information Centre, 9 Koroneou Str, 71202 Iraklion. Tel: 30 81 22 90 13.

Other useful addresses
Ministry of National Economy, Department of Private Investment Promotion and Evaluation, Platia Syntagmatos, Athens.

British Embassy, 1 Ploutarchou Street, Athens 139.

International Chamber of Commerce, 27 Chaning Street, Athens.

British Hellenic Chamber of Commerce, 4 Valaoritou Street, Athens.

The Embassy of Greece, 1a Holland Park, London, W11.

Ministry of Commerce, Kaningos Square, 106 77 Athens.

Department of Trade and Industry – Greek Desk, 1–19 Victoria Street, London, SW1H 0ET. Tel: 071 215 4776.

Portugal

European information centres

Eurogabinete, Associao Industrial Portuense, Avenida da Boavists 2671, P-4102 Porto Codex. Tel: 351 2 677322.

Eurogabinete, Banco de Fomento Nacional, Av Casal Pibeiro 59, P-1000 Lisboa. Tel: 351 1 561071/532055.

Commissao de Coordenacao da Regiao do Algavre, European Information Centre, Praca da Liberdade 2, 8000 Faro. Tel: 351 80 2401/27456.

Other useful addresses

Institute for Foreign Commerce (ICEP), Av de Liberdade, 258 Lisbon.

National Registry of Legal Persons (RNPC), Praca Silvestre Pinheiro Ferreira, 1-C Lisboa.

The Embassy of Portugal, 11 Belgrave Square, London, SW1.

Department of Trade and Industry – Portuguese Desk, 1–19 Victoria Street, London, SW1H 0ET. Tel: 071 215 5307.

(Notary) Rua dos Douradores, 135-20, Lisboa.

(Notary) Rua da Prata, 199-20 E, Lisboa.

(Notary) Av Guerra Junqueiro, 21-10, Lisboa.

Denmark

European information centres

EF-Radgivningskontoret for Fyn, European Information Centre, Norregade 51, DK-5000 Odense C. Tel: 45 9 146030.

Dansk Teknisk Oplysningstjeneste, European Information Centre, Ryggards Alle 131 A, Postbox 1992, 2820 Copenhagen. Tel: 45 31 20 90 92.

Haandvaerraadet, European Information Centre, L1 Sct Hansgade 20, 8800 Viborg. Tel: 45 86 62 92 99.

Other useful addresses

Information Office for Foreign Investment in Denmark, 25 Sondergade, DK-8600 Silkeborg. Tel: 45 6 82 56 55.

Ministry of Industry, 12 Slotsholmsgade, DK-1216 Copenhagen K. Tel: 45 1 12 11 97.

Danish Bankers Association, 7 Amaliegade, DK-1256 Copenhagen K. Tel: 45 1 12 02 00.

The Association of State-Authorised Public Accountants, 8 Kronprinsessgade, DK-1306 Copenhagen K. Tel: 45 1 12 91 91.

Federation of Danish Industries, 18 H C Andersens Boulevard, DK-1596 Copenhagen V. Tel: 45 1 15 22 33.

Danish Commerce and Companies Agency – Aktieselskabs Registeret, Kampmannsgade 1, 1604 Copenhagen K.

The Embassy of Denmark, 55 Sloane Street, London, SW1.

Information Office for Foreign Investment in Denmark, 25 Sondergade, DK-8600 Silkeborg. Tel: 45 8 682 5655.

The Dutch Chamber of Commerce, Grosserer Societetet, Borsen DK-1217, Copenhagen K. Tel: 45 3 315 3320.

Danish Ministry of Foreign Affairs: Investeringssekretariatet H.I., Asiatisk Plads 2, DK-1448 Copenhagen K. Tel: 45 33 92 00 00.

Registry of Companies: Aktieselskabs Registeret, Kampmannsgade 1, 1604 Copenhagen K. Tel: 01 12 42 80.

Copenhagen HandelsBank AS, International Trade Promotion, 2 Holmes Kanal, DK-1091 Copenhagen K.

British Chamber of Commerce: Det Danske Handelskammer, Borsen, DK-1217 Copenhagen K.

Republic of Ireland

European information centres
Irish Export Board/Coras Trachtala, European Information Centre, Merrion Hall, PO Box 203, Strand Road, Sandymount, Dublin 4. Tel: 353 1 695011.

Cork Chamber of Commerce, European Information Centre, Fitzgerald House, Summerhill, Cork. Tel: 353 21 50 90 44.

Galway Chamber of Commerce and Industry, European Information Centre, Hynes Buildings, St Augustine Street, Galway. Tel: 353 91 98127.

Company formation offices
Companies Registration Office, Lower Castle Yard, Dublin Castle, Dublin 2.

Other useful addresses
The Embassy of Ireland, 17 Grosvenor Place, London, SW1.

Industrial Development Authority, Ireland House, 150 New Bond Street, London, W1Y 0DH.

British Embassy, 33 Merrion Road, Dublin 4.

Industrial Development Authority of Ireland (IDA), Wilton Park House, Wilton Place, Dublin 2. Tel: 0001 686633.

Luxembourg

European information centres
Euroguichet, Chambre de Commerce du Grand Duche de Luxembourg. Tel: 352 453853.

Chambre des Metiers du Grand-Duche de Luxembourg, European Information Centre, 41 Rue Glesener, 1631 Luxembourg. Tel: 352 400022 1.

Other useful addresses
Ministère de L'Economie et des Classes Moyennes, La Boite Postale 97, 2010 Luxembourg Ville.

Register de Commerce, Palais de Justice, Ancien Batiment, Rue du Palais de Justice, L-1841 Luxembourg.

The Embassy of Luxembourg, 27 Wilton Crescent, London, SW1.

Chambre de Commerce, Du Grande-Duche de Luxembourg, 7 rue Alcide de Gasperi, L-2981 Luxembourg. Tel: 352 435 853.

(establishment permit) Ministry of Small and Medium Size Enterprises, 19–21 boulevard Royal, L-2910 Luxembourg. Tel: 352 4794 517.

(business register) Court of Justice, Registre de Commerce, 12 Cote d'Eich, L-1450 Luxembourg. Tel: 352 475981 440.

(work permits) Employment Administration, 34 avenue de la Porte Neuve, L-2227 Luxembourg. Tel: 352 47 68 55 1.

(tax formalities) Tax and Excise Administration, 45 boulevard Roosevelt, L-2982 Luxembourg. Tel: 352 40 45 1.

(social security) Common Centre of Social Security, 125 route d'Esch, L-1471 Luxembourg. Tel: 352 49 92 01.

The Mercury titles on the pages that follow may also be of interest. All Mercury books are available from booksellers or, in case of difficulty, from:

Mercury Books
Gold Arrow Publications Ltd
862 Garratt Lane
London SW17 0NB

Further details and the complete catalogue of Mercury business books are also available from the above address.

COMPETITION AND BUSINESS REGULATION IN THE SINGLE MARKET
S J Berwin & Co.

EC company law and competition policy have a pivotal role in the political and legislative initiatives leading to the single market in 1992. They both define the relevant legislative framework for the completion of the internal market and ensure that the agreed rules will be fully and effectively applied throughout the EC for the benefit of all businesses, small and large alike.

EC company law sets down minimum standards and allows companies and firms to penetrate EC markets and establish themselves without barriers or restrictions, thereby facilitating intra-Community trade and cooperation; while EC competition rules establish conditions of free and effective competition in the single market to ensure that anti-competitive practices do not create new barriers to trade or other forms of protectionism.

This book examines the impact of EC company law and competition rules from the point of view of British businesses and explains how these rules create a new dynamic legal environment leading both to organic growth and growth in partnership with other EC companies and firms. Case studies illustrate how, in practice, an awareness and understanding of Community law rules enables businesses to take full advantage of the single market while limiting their exposure to the numerous legal pitfalls along the way.

From its inception, S J Berwin & Co, one of the fastest growing firms of solicitors in the UK, recognised the importance of the EC and established a group responsible for the specialised practice of Community law. In addition, all members of the firm advise on Community law: how it relates to competition, company law, mergers and acquisitions, financial services and banking, taxation, anti-dumping, intellectual property rights, pharmaceuticals and the free movement of goods and services. S J Berwin maintains close contacts with EC officials to ensure that the firm has at its disposal the most accurate and up-to-date information on legal and policy documents.

- Successful hardback sale of over 3700 copies
- Aimed at the 1992 market, of which there will be increasing awareness during the year
- Completely updated

ISBN 1 85252 195 3 (paperback)

£9.99

PRESENTING YOUR CASE TO EUROPE

Peter Danton de Rouffignac

Increasingly companies and organisations are finding a need to present their case more effectively to the various Community institutions. This applies equally to those wishing to influence the course of European legislation, to apply for Community funding, to attract investment to their city or region, or simply to put across the viewpoint of a trade organisation or pressure group. In each case there is a need for a sound knowledge of how the community works, where and when important information is available to the outsider, where the power really lies, and what can be done to influence the European decision-making process.

Assuming little prior knowledge, this book provides a step-by-step guide to the European Community institutions, and shows how policy decisions are arrived at and funds allocated. It examines how national governments monitor Community legislation, and provides a number of case studies showing how powerful organisations representing employers, trade unions or special interests carry out their lobbying role. A final section includes an A to Z of lobbying techniques that will help any organisation present its case more effectively to the politicians and bureaucrats.

Peter Danton de Rouffignac is a consultant specialising in European affairs and advises organisations on how to research and present their case to Brussels. He is the author of more than a dozen business books and reports on both West and East Europe and lectures at a number of colleges and universities on European affairs. He is a member of the Institute of Public Relations and of the European Association of Public Relations Consultants.

- The first comprehensive guide to the apparent maze of 'Eurobureaucracy'

- Essential for people who want to influence EC decision-making (it can be done!)

- Written by an acknowledged expert

ISBN 1 85251 083 8 (hardback)   £25.00

THE ECU, THE EMS AND EUROPE'S FINANCIAL MARKETS

Alain Jean

First published in French, this important book is a complete and authoritative guide to the European Monetary System.

The author first describes the principles, functioning, enhancements, weaknesses and drawbacks of the EMS and discusses the report, originally known as the Delors Plan, which has been considerably extended by the committee of governors of the central banks of the member States of the European Community.

In part two, he analyses the function of the ecu, and its financial and commercial use. He emphasises the positive aspects of the use of the ecu in financial markets as well as its growing commercial importance. He explains in detail how the European compensation system operates, how the private ecu is controlled and how these official actions are important in the development of the different markets for the private ecu.

The author, Alain Jean, who has a doctorate in monetary economics, is an economist at the Ecu Banking Association. The EBA is charged, along with the Bank of International Settlements, with the organisation and day-to-day functioning of the compensation system and control of the private ecu.

'Should merit the attention of a huge public.'
Governor of the Bank of France

'Will certainly contribute to the development of monetary Europe.'
Governor of the Bank of Spain

'An excellent analysis.' Institut Monetair Luxembourgeois

ISBN 1 85251 145 1 (hardback)   £25.00